Why Walk When You Can Fly?

Soar Beyond Your Fears and Love Yourself and Others Unconditionally

By
Isha

16
EasyRead Large

Copyright Page from the Original Book

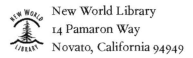 New World Library
14 Pamaron Way
Novato, California 94949

Text design by Tona Pearce Myers

Library of Congress Cataloging-in-Publication Data
Isha.
  Why walk when you can fly? : soar beyond your fears and love your-self and others unconditionally / Isha.
     p.   cm.
ISBN 978-1-57731-637-4 (pbk. : alk. paper)
  1. Self-realization. 2. Conduct of life. 3. Fear. 4. Love. 5. Spiritual life.
I. Title.
BF637.S4I84 2009
158—dc22   2008033003

First printing, November 2008
ISBN 978-1-57731-637-4
Printed in Canada on 100% postconsumer-waste recycled paper

New World Library is a proud member of the Green Press Initiative.

10   9   8   7   6   5   4   3   2   1

TABLE OF CONTENTS

Praise for Why Walk When You Can Fly?

"The facets explained in this book vibrate on an enlightened level of being and provide a practical way to apply the findings of my research: that the nature of our thoughts profoundly affects our experience of life. In *Why Walk When You Can Fly?* you will learn a simple system to go inward and begin to transform your perception from one based in fear to one based in love and unity in the present moment."

—Masaru Emoto, author of *The Hidden Messages in Water*

"Isha teaches with warmth and creativity, sharing stories and anecdotes that help us know that we too can take this journey to our deep heart. Through her practices and suggestions, Isha gives us courage to live fully in this circle of love that is our lasting connection with our true selves."

—Meredith L. Young-Sowers, DDiv, author of *Spirit Heals* and *Agartha*

"This is an important, even essential book. We live in a time when millions are being called to spread their wings and fly, bringing into manifestation a world that reflects our highest dreams. The only barrier is fear, and Isha gives practical ways to release fear's hold over our lives."

—James F. Twyman, author of *The Moses Code*

Great teachers are eternal students—to my mother, with love iv

Introduction

Once there was a king who received a gift of two magnificent falcons from Arabia. They were pere- grine falcons, the most beautiful birds he had ever seen. He gave the precious birds to his head falconer to be trained.

Months passed, and one day the head falconer in- formed the king that though one of the falcons was flying majestically, soaring high in the sky, the other bird had not moved from its branch since the day it had arrived.

The king summoned healers and sorcerers from all the land to tend to the falcon, but no one could make the bird fly. He presented the task to the members of his court, but the next day, the king saw through the palace window that the bird had still not moved from its perch. Having tried every- thing else, the king thought to himself, "Maybe I need someone more familiar with the countryside to understand the nature of this problem." So he cried out to his court, "Go and get a farmer!"

In the morning, the king was thrilled to see the falcon soaring high above the palace gardens. He said to his court, "Bring me the doer of this mira- cle."

The court quickly located the farmer, who came and stood before the king. The king asked him, "How did you make the falcon fly?"

With his head bowed, the farmer said to the king, "It was easy, your highness. I simply cut the branch."

We were all made to fly—to realize our incredible potential as human beings. But instead of doing that, we sit on our branches, clinging to the things that are familiar to us. The possibilities are endless, but for most of us, they remain undiscovered. We conform to the familiar, the comfortable, the mundane. So for the most part, our lives are mediocre instead of exciting, thrilling, fulfilling.

I am like the farmer in this story. I am here to offer you an insight that, if you apply it, will cut whatever branch you are clinging to and cause you to soar.

In this book, I am going to teach you a system that will destroy the branch of fear you cling to, freeing you to the glory of flight. This system is called the Isha System, and I have witnessed tens of thousands of lives change through its practice.

The first aspect of the system takes the form of four *facets,* which make up what we call the *Diamond Portal*—the experience of our perfection, the state of permanent peace and love. These facets are simple statements of profound truths, pure expressions of unconditional love, which we will repeat to ourselves mentally without any strain or effort. Each facet represents an aspect of the experience of union and is designed to produce the vibration of unity. By practicing the facets, we will begin to create radical inner change, moving away from the fear-based habits and insecurities that keep us from flying.

The facets of the Isha System may seem extremely simple, but in reality they are extraordinarily powerful and transformative tools for inner growth. They bring individuals rapidly into the experience of their true natures—the experience of what we call *love-consciousness.*

Love-consciousness is not to be confused with the "consciousness" of psychology. It does not refer to the conscious mind as opposed to the unconscious mind. Love-consciousness is the unconditional love within all beings, an experience that keeps expanding when we dive deep within ourselves. It is not a strange or ethereal experience but something very concrete and natural; you have probably experienced it before in moments of your life—maybe while spending time with a baby, expressing yourself creatively, watching the sun set, or meditating.

For most of us, the unconscious mind is made up of the fears and doubts that keep us clinging to our branch, but instead of analyzing every aspect of those self-defeating patterns, with the Isha System we simply focus on the love. Then everything that comes from fear will start to fade away.

In modern society, most of us tend to think that if something is easy, it is worthless; the maxim "no pain, no gain" summarizes this perspective. Some of us believe that the only way to achieve freedom is through concentrating earnestly while meditating in complex and uncomfortable positions. Others have been told by their parents or by certain religions that suffering is the way to liberation. Since the facets of the Isha System are effortless and painless, they don't fit with these beliefs about how to reach self-realization.

The facets bring us into the moment. There is nothing complicated about that. They are simple, just as the secret to happiness is simple, just as love and joy are simple. All those things come from innocence—that is, the capacity to be fully present. Innocence is one of the cornerstones of the Isha System. Children exemplify innocence perfectly: they aren't complex; they aren't planning for the future or lamenting the past; they just are.

Do you remember when you were a child? You were happy for no reason. You lived perfectly in the moment. You found magic in everything. Life was a joy. You didn't judge yourself. You thought you were perfect exactly as you were. If you were happy, you laughed. If you were sad, you cried. And if you were angry, you stamped your foot, and then you were happy again. As you practice this system, I want you to become that child again. I want you to embrace that simplicity and spontaneity and let go of the questions, controls, and opinions of the intellect. If you can rekindle the lost innocence of childhood while at the same time maintaining the maturity and sense of responsibility you have gained from adulthood, this simple system will work rapidly and profoundly, transforming your life in ways you can't imagine.

We'll begin the journey by exploring the facets. Each of the first four chapters addresses one of them. Along with the specific instructions about how to use the facets, I include universal spiritual lessons to help you see your life more clearly. These spiritual truths will guide you as you begin to work with the facets in your life. Chapter 5 gives you more practical advice on how to incorporate the facets into your life and addresses common experiences you may have while using the facets. Chapter 6 describes the seven components of the Isha System, the facets being the first component. This will give you the broader framework into which the facets fit. As you work with the facets and the rest of the System, you'll notice great insights and changes emerging in your life. Chapter 7, the final one in the book, will give you guidelines on how to integrate these shifts into the overall picture of your life. It also includes the stories of several people whom I've worked with as they embraced the Isha System.

I believe you'll find, as they did, that the System will help you to see the world—and yourself—through the lens of love-consciousness and discover a deep, abiding peace.

Part 1

The Isha Facets

Chapter 1

The First Facet

Embracing the Present Moment

A newlywed couple moved to an apartment in a very busy neighborhood. On the first morning in their new home, after she had made coffee, the young bride looked through the window and watched her neighbor hanging sheets out to dry. "What dirty sheets!" she thought to herself. "Maybe she needs to buy a different kind of detergent. I should go and teach her how to wash them properly." Every few days, she muttered the same thing to her husband with disdain while watching her neighbor hanging out the dirty laundry in the early-morning light.

A month passed, and one day the young wife was surprised to see that her neighbor was hanging out perfectly clean sheets. She exclaimed to her husband, "Look! She finally learned to wash her clothes. I wonder who taught her how."

The husband replied, "Well, in reality, darling, the only difference is that I got up early this morning and cleaned the window."

Each of us has been looking through a window all our lives. Tainted by the beliefs and ideas we have adopted from the past, its distorted surface creates our world and governs our perception of the universe. In most cases, our windows are covered in the grime and dust of a lifetime, clouding our vision, blocking the light of the truth from view.

The window of the mind becomes dirty when the subconscious is full of self-criticism and fear-based opinions. Unfortunately, this is the case for many of us—erratic, incessant thoughts are our constant companions. Our adult minds are in perpetual chaos and contradiction. Our thoughts jostle endlessly for our attention, as we jump from one distraction to another. This incessant thinking affects our entire nervous system.

How does it do this? The answer lies in vibration. Our thoughts have a vibration, just as any sound has a vibration. Those vibrations resound within the nervous system, affecting our inner vibratory rate. When our thoughts are erratic and conflictive, they create a dissonant vibration in the body. When our thoughts are harmonious and creative, the vibration of union envelops us, and everything that is not vibrating in that frequency begins to fall away naturally.

The Restlessness of Humanity

We seldom feel complete in the present moment. In the modern world, people at all levels of society and in every walk of life struggle with a feeling of underlying dissatisfaction and unrest. We often find ourselves yearning for something more—no matter what we have achieved in our lives, the fulfillment we so desire remains elusive.

Many of us find that our attention constantly gravitates toward what is wrong with our lives. We hardly ever focus on appreciating all the wonderful things we have; instead we habitually criticize our surroundings, blaming the outside for our discontent. We are seldom in the present moment long enough to embrace the magic of the now.

I have always been an overachiever, putting all my heart into everything I do. But for much of my life, it was never enough. I felt dissatisfied with myself, always expecting more. Incapable of fully appreciating the things I had accomplished, I was incessantly focused on what was missing.

In fact, although I appeared to be a powerful, successful, and confident woman, deep down I always doubted myself. I criticized myself constantly, and although I was not aware of it, beneath my self-assured personality lay a great deal of fear.

To some extent, we all experience this disillusionment. No matter where we are on this planet, we can feel discontented, though we blame our inner torment on our location or circumstances. It can happen in our great cities; despite all the constant distractions of our push-button world and the pervasive presence of people in our metropolises, individuals die of deep depression and loneliness right in the heart of places like Manhattan and Buenos Aires. And it can happen in the country, to those surrounded only by the natural world and the people they love. Wherever we are, we feel intense regret, guilt, and pain as a result of things that have happened in our lives, and we yearn for things we wish would happen. This is the insanity of the human condition—our minds' tendency to always be dwelling on the past or projecting into the future, thereby making us miserable.

Most of us have an idea of how happiness should look. We tend to see happiness as a future moment—when we can afford a bigger house, when we can buy a new car, when we find the perfect partner, when the children grow up, when we retire.

Have you noticed that when you achieve your goals—the better job, the bigger house, the new partner—there is always something more for you to set your heart on? It seems that no matter what we achieve, fulfillment is always beyond our grasp. Why is nothing ever enough?

We are waiting for *something* to happen, anything that might bring us the satisfaction that has eluded us for so long. The future seems to hold our only hope for true fulfillment, while the present moment—where we are all along, without any effort—is where we least expect to find it.

What prevents us from discovering the beauty of life lived in the now? The cause is not external, as we may have often thought, but internal. It lies within our own minds.

The Matrix of the Mind

The intellect is one of the great treasures of the human experience. It provides the means for constant evolution. Scientific discoveries and recent advances in communication and technology pay homage to its brilliance, and on a more personal level, it provides essential abilities, such as discernment and comparison, to help us make decisions in our daily lives.

Yet the scope of the mind, although varied and fascinating, is limited. It cannot fully understand the complexities of love, for example. Instead, it tends to focus on the mundane and flits incessantly from thought to thought. Even in the midst of great beauty—watching the sun set over a golden hillside, for example—the mind wanders to other times, other places...

"Wow! That sunset is amazing. They say a sunset like this means we'll have a clear day tomorrow. I sure hope so, because it's my only day off and I have so much to do. I should really go to the gym first thing in the morning—I've got to lose some weight! And then I have to go to the hardware store to buy paint, do laundry, get the house ready for the guests to arrive, and figure out what to cook for dinner. The last time we had people over, they really liked that pasta dish—maybe I should make that again. Too bad the birthday cake our friends brought over that time was terrible. Oh no! Mom's birthday is tomorrow, and I forgot to send a card. I'm a terrible daughter...."

By identifying so deeply with the constant chattering of the mind, we have lost sight of all that lies beyond its constraints: our true greatness, buried there beneath the mind's limiting thoughts and opinions. When this happens, the mind becomes a *matrix.*

We are ensnared in this mental matrix. It is like a net that we get trapped in, and we imagine that the net is all there is. We find ourselves stuck in the limited ways of thinking we learned in childhood.

Because of the limiting beliefs of this mental matrix, it's easier for us to listen to someone telling us that we are just average, ordinary, or nothing special than it is to hear that we are capable of greatness. Many of us believe that we aren't as good as other people. From early childhood, we were told that we were inadequate, not up to the task, or even stupid.

I certainly didn't escape the matrix when I was growing up. Living in Melbourne, Australia, in my school years I was much taller than most of the kids my age. My height made me an excellent runner, and I easily outran my competitors in any race. My teachers would say to me, "Don't win by so much. You make the other children feel bad." As a result of this, I began to hold back some of my ability. I put the brakes on myself. I started to believe that I was meant not to shine but only to be "normal."

A bit later, the teachers in my all-women's college frowned on my extroverted behavior. They felt that a young lady ought to be unassuming and demure, never standing out from the crowd, never in a starring role. I was so desperate for their approval that I became insecure. With time, I adopted their opinion as my own and figured there must be something wrong with me since I wasn't the quiet, passive young woman they thought I should be. I learned to doubt myself all the time. I began to act small.

Instead of soaring aloft, taking in the magnificence and beauty of life, most of us act small. We simply don't see our greatness, so we embody the poor sense of ourselves we internalized from our family, schooling, and society in general. As a consequence, we are all walking around in a haze, searching incessantly for peace, love, and happiness.

We yearn for absolute freedom. We want to fly like the falcon. We want to be all we can be, but instead we cling to the branch of mediocrity.

We have bought into the matrix of the mind, as if the way we *think* of ourselves is all we really are.

Duality and Its Contrasts

The matrix of the mind is always trying to intellectualize and understand. It is always focused on good versus bad, right versus wrong. In fact, good, bad, right, and wrong are the building blocks of the matrix. It sees everything from the point of view of *duality,* or separation. It boxes the world into categories, labeling everything and everyone around us. To some extent, these labels allow us to experience human life, but when they become our only means of perception and we consider them to be the absolute truth, we lose the innocence that delights in the wonder of existence.

Our perception of the physical universe is full of contrasts and separations. We see abundance and we see famine. We see the atrocities of war and the selfless giving of visionaries such as Gandhi or Mother Teresa. We see all sorts of different things, creating separation and disparity as well as both tragedy and joy. Full of contrast, the world forms an incredible landscape of diversity and wonder.

Yet when we perceive all this richness through the matrix of the intellect, all the divisions make us feel vulnerable, separate, small. We identify with the distinctions so strongly that we lose sight of the vibrant beauty of the big picture. The consequence is that we are superficial. We are stuck in the intellect, immersed in the constraints of the mind. Being mired in the matrix causes us to float on the surface of life instead of going deep—and so we fail to find the fulfillment we seek.

The Comfort of Limitation

Although the clouded perception that the matrix of the intellect has given us makes us numb to the fullness that exists in every moment, we have found a certain comfort within its boundaries. It is a space defined by all our fears and limitations, but within its constraints is everything we know, everything we believe, everything we have come to trust. There, our past experiences rule our every move.

Because there is a certain comfort in the place we have claimed for ourselves, to embrace our greatness—to believe that we *deserve* to live to our full potential—is the hardest thing for us to do. Even when we have dreams that we would like to fulfill, it's difficult for us to move out of our comfort zones. We want results, we hope for good things, we even look for opportunities—but are we willing to let go of what we are accustomed to in order to achieve our heart's desire?

Those who seek change allow themselves to fly. Those who feel inadequate cling to the branch. Which are you?

If you are clinging to the branch, what are you holding on to that stops you from flying? What will you not let go of?

Cutting the Branch

We are about to learn the first Isha facet, the first of four extremely powerful tools that will help us cut the branch of the fear-based habits of the past, so that we can find our wings and the glory of flight.

In order to benefit from the full power of these facets, it is necessary to commit to regular practice. If we join a gym but never go, we do not get fitter. In the same way, if we do not practice the facets, they do not work. Ideally, practice for an hour a day with the eyes closed. You can divide this hour into two blocks of half an hour or three blocks of twenty minutes. The most important thing is that you do it. If on some days you can't do an hour, a shorter time is better than nothing.

This process works on a very profound level, and for most people the changes are immediate. They experience a peace and joy that grow deeper as they continue practicing. Yet for some people, it takes a few days or even weeks of regular practice to start seeing the changes. Some find that their friends notice the changes before they do. Even if they are a little skeptical as to what is happening within them, they find people coming up to them and saying, "You look different today," or, "You've changed. What have you been doing?"

I recommend that you continue practicing the facets regularly for a minimum of four weeks, no matter what happens while you are practicing. In my experience, four weeks of regular practice is enough for anyone to appreciate enormous benefits.

Another important thing to bear in mind when you are learning these facets is to be innocent, open, and non-judgmental toward the practice. The experience of these facets will be unlike anything you have ever done before, and the more open you are, the easier it will be for you to adopt this new perspective and experience the benefits. At first, using the facets might appear to be like other spiritual or self-improvement practices, but give the facets an opportunity to work their magic in your life, and you'll discover that they are different from anything you've ever experienced.

The First Facet

In each moment, there is perfection to be found. When we are totally present, nothing is wrong; all the apparent imperfections appear when we stray off into the past or the future. The first facet will bring us into the perfection of this moment. By bringing our attention fully into the present, the first facet naturally draws our awareness into the experience of love-consciousness.

Being in the present does not mean that we will not continue to grow. Life is always evolving, always moving toward greater growth and expansion. Yet by embracing the inherent perfection of this moment, we naturally elevate our internal vibration, re-creating ourselves in ever-higher frequencies of love.

Bringing our attention fully into the present destroys one of humanity's most deep-seated negative beliefs. This belief is the origin of our discontent. It is a false mental idea that keeps us from experiencing fulfillment. It is the idea that *there is something wrong with this moment.* Deep down, although we may not be aware of it, almost all of us share this belief. Even if we love our lives, very few of us feel absolutely complete.

The first facet brings us to that completion by healing this belief at its source. When we make this profound change deep in our subconscious, our entire perception of life shifts dramatically. Through the use of this facet, you will be amazed that something so simple can have such an incredible impact on your life.

We are now going to create a perfectly harmonious thought, a profound truth that reaches beyond all the negative conditioning of the intellect, anchoring us in the beauty of the here and now. This thought is focused on the concept of *love* as an all-encompassing force of unity. It will use the emotion of *praise,* which simply means appreciation. When we shift our perception to appreciation, we begin to take the power away from our old fear-based beliefs and habits and move toward more love, toward love-consciousness. The more we choose the love, the more we clean our window, until the light of pure awareness shines through its crystal-clear surface. We move away from our perception of criticism and self-doubt, free to fly high in joyful celebration of the here and now. Here is that thought, the first facet:

Praise love for this moment in its perfection.

Here's how to practice the first facet:

1. Sit comfortably and close your eyes. Allow any thoughts that come to mind to gently pass. Don't seek to stop your thoughts; don't try to enter a state of no-mind. Instead, just allow whatever comes to happen naturally.

2. Say, in your mind, this thought: *Praise love for this moment in its perfection.* Think it without any effort, the same way you might think any other thought, without concentrating or even trying to understand its meaning.

3. At the same time that you think this facet, put your attention deep in the area of your heart.

4. After thinking the facet, leave a space, a pause. After a few moments, repeat the thought and again leave a space.

5. Continue in this way for about twenty minutes. You can glance at your watch or a clock to check the time.

Don't think the facet over and over again nonstop as you would a mantra—always leave a space of a few seconds between each repetition. You may experience peace and silence during this gap, but it is also possible that you will have thoughts. Sometimes you may forget the facet, change some of the words, or stray from the point of attention. If this happens, as soon as you realize it, simply go back to thinking the facet correctly. All of this is perfectly normal and natural. Just remember: when you realize that you are not thinking the facet, choose to think it again.

Also, the quality of the thoughts you have in the gap between each repetition may vary widely. You may think, "Isn't life wonderful? Aren't these facets great? Isn't this system fantastic?" Or you might think, "This is such a waste of time! Why am I even bothering? How could such a ridiculous little phrase have any effect on my life?" And that is also fine. The facets will work, irrespective of the thoughts you may have during practice.

One of the things I most love about these facets is that they work automatically. You need not believe in them in order to experience their benefits. This is what makes them so effective—because our fears are habitual, we need a tool that will automatically create a new experience, even if our thoughts are resisting it. The important thing is that you have your own experience. Only through practice will you come to appreciate the benefits of the facets, not because I am telling you about them, but because you will see the changes within yourself.

Bear in mind that the Isha facets have a very specific structure that should not be changed; if you change them, the facets will lose their effectiveness. Do not change a facet so that it feels more comfortable for you—many people have a resistance to the word *praise,* for example. *Praise* simply means appreciation, and the profound effects of each part of this phrase, including *praise,* reach far beyond our surface reactions to them. And any resistance we may feel will dissolve as we continue to practice.

We refer to practicing the facets as *unifying.* There are two ways to unify: with eyes open and with eyes closed. Keeping the eyes closed is the most profound way to unify, as it takes you deep into the experience of love-consciousness.

You can think this facet with your eyes open whenever you want, in any situation. For maximum results, think it every time you remember—while you are brushing your teeth, exercising at the gym, watching TV, or waiting in line at the bank. Every time you use the facets, you are bringing your attention completely into the present moment and connecting with love-con-sciousness. When you are present in the moment, the projections and fears clouding your window of perception begin to dissolve. You start to see with new eyes.

You will find that all areas of your life will benefit from unifying. Doing so during the day with the eyes open brings enhanced mental clarity, a deeper experience of peace, and as a result, self-trust. You will become more efficient, more relaxed, and less stressed in all situations just by using the facets with your eyes open. Many people find that using the facets with the eyes open helps them concentrate while studying or working—they become more effective, accomplishing more in less time.

Tonight, before you go to sleep, unify for twenty minutes with your eyes closed. You can do it sitting or lying down—practice in whatever position is comfortable for you. You can start practicing for an hour a day with your eyes closed—in two sessions of half an hour or three sessions of twenty minutes. As we go on learning the other facets in this book, we will learn how to incorporate them into this hour.

What You May Feel While Unifying

How did you feel while you were unifying? Maybe you felt peaceful or relaxed. Maybe you had lots of thoughts, or maybe you hardly had any. Maybe you felt joyful, sad, or even a little bit angry. Maybe you had memories of your childhood or felt energy running through your body. Maybe you felt pain in old injuries. Maybe you felt sleepy. Or maybe you didn't feel anything at all. Many things can happen when we are unifying, and for now, just know that they are all perfect. We never look for a specific experience when we unify—we just embrace whatever happens naturally. The following experiences are common for those who are new to unifying.

Remember to think the facet: Praise love for this moment in its perfection.

(Attention: deep in the heart)

EMOTIONS CONTRARY TO THE FACET

While practicing a facet, you may well feel the exact opposite of what the facet represents, but this will not impede the changes that are taking place deep within you. While using the first facet, for example, you may feel resentful or frustrated about your current circumstances. Don't fight this if it happens—it is important that you do not try to control the sensations or emotions that arise.

HEIGHTENED SENSES

Another possibility is that you may experience a heightening in your senses while unifying. You might become more sensitive to noise, for example, or smell. This state of increased alertness is a result of the expansion of love-consciousness. As you become more conscious, you become increasingly aware of the subtle aspects of the world around you. This is also perfect.

PHYSICAL PAIN

You may also find that you feel pain in your body while you are unifying. Your muscles might ache as a result of accumulated tension being released. You may relive symptoms of illnesses from childhood or feel pain in old injuries. This does not mean your injury or illness is coming back; on the contrary, it means your body is completing the healing that was previously left unfinished, and the result will be better health and greater physical wellbeing. Just keep unifying, and remind yourself that you are healing. The discomfort will undoubtedly leave very quickly, and you will return to a state of peace and calm.

THIRST

You might find that you feel thirsty during and after unifying. It is important to drink a lot of water when unifying, to help flush out the toxins that are being released. We will explore this in more depth later.

The First Step on the Path

Although I had been meditating for many years, through practicing the first facet I came to realize how blind I really was to the sheer wonder and beauty of the world. When I lived in Melbourne, Australia, I used to walk my dog along the seafront. Eternally busy and overachieving, I hurried along with her leash wrapped around my arm, my cell phone wedged between my jawbone and my shoulder, talking frantically, cigarette in one hand, coffee in the other.

Remember to think a facet as you read: Praise love for this moment in its perfection. (Attention: deep in the heart)

When I began to experience love-consciousness, I was walking my dog one day without my habitual accessories. Suddenly I heard an unfamiliar, repetitive sound. I paused and listened. It was a sound I had never heard before—the sound of the waves lapping on the shore.

It was a moment of intense realization. I had walked my dog along this beachfront every day for five years, yet I had never heard the sound of the ocean! I had been so lost in my thoughts, my concerns, and my anxieties that I had been completely deaf to the call of the sea. In that moment, I realized that I had never been in the present moment before.

Normally, our thoughts are constantly taking us outward, to future concerns and the regrets of the past. We are so immersed in the intellect that we are never with ourselves long enough to realize that everything we are searching for so desperately is already here.

This facet is the first step on the path to living in the moment. As we start to expand love-consciousness, we learn to embrace the now, instead of frantically trying to change and control everything in our lives. We learn to flow within the ever-changing experience of life.

The Power of Choice

I have always been fascinated by two council workers who tend the gardens along the riverbank in Santiago, Chile. Their story illustrates perfectly how much we lose by clinging to the ideas of our intellects, and how much we can gain by letting go of the ranting of the mind and anchoring our awareness in love-consciousness.

One of the council workers is an elderly woman. She is an expression of pure grace. She has refined features and posture. The question, "Why is she working here?" comes to mind when you see her. At first, she seems misplaced, but soon you realize that she belongs everywhere. She has a serenity, an inner peace that radiates across the garden like sunlight. She is so loving within her work, it is as if she is caressing the leaves as she sweeps them from her path. The runners on the trail pass by her unnoticed, like a breeze—nothing can cast a shadow on her moment or distract her from her job.

The other gardener is an old man whom time has pained to such an extent that it is impossible for him to be present with himself in any moment. He hastily scurries along the path with a bag of leaves in his hand, constantly looking at his watch, sweating profusely, distracted in his own compulsions. And when he sees me, he frantically asks the same question every day. He looks at me with desperation and asks, "Lady, lady, what's the time?" I always answer, but he doesn't wait to listen: he hurries off before he can hear me and asks the next person on the trail the same question. He doesn't want the answer—he just wants to be anywhere but with himself. Chasing time, chasing answers, avoiding *being*—to such a point that he has gone a little mad.

The distinction between these two people is glaring. One is a perfect picture of a person living in oneness; the other a perfect picture of someone who is trapped in the matrix of his mind. Both people are in the same place, doing the same thing. Yet it is not what they are doing that governs their happiness—rather, it is what they are being. Every time you think a facet, you are choosing what you want to be. You are choosing to be the love instead of identifying with the interminable unrest of the mind.

Keeping Your Dreams

At first, living in the moment and achieving your dreams may sound somewhat contradictory. How can we focus on our goals without going off into the future? But being in the moment does not mean we don't plan our lives; it simply means that we let go of the concerns and preoccupations that keep us from opening our wings and discovering the freedom of flight.

Normally, the limitations of the mind keep us from achieving our dreams. But when we relinquish our fear-based thought patterns, our dreams spontaneously become our reality. By removing the idea that there is something wrong with this moment, this facet shakes the foundations of our subconscious fears. Then the entire edifice of self-doubt and separation we have built throughout our lives falls into a heap of rubble. We are no longer constrained by the limits of our past, and nothing is left to stop us from reaching for our dreams.

There once lived a boy whose father was a poor horse trainer. His father enjoyed his job but barely made enough money to support his family. One day at school, the boy was given an assignment to write about what he would like to be when he grew up. That night, he excitedly wrote a seven-page essay, describing his dream of one day owning a horse stud so that he could breed his own horses. He wrote the essay with great care and attention to detail. He even drew a plan of the land and the house he dreamed of owning. He put his whole heart into the project.

The next day, he handed his project to his teacher. When he received it back, he had been awarded an F, and his teacher had written at the top of the essay in red, "See me after class."

The boy stayed behind when the bell rang and asked his teacher, "Why did you give me an F?"

The teacher replied, "Your essay described an unrealistic future for a boy like you. You have no money of your own, and your family is poor. You don't have the resources to buy your own horse stud. You would have to buy land and your original stock, and on top of that, there would be maintenance costs. There is no way you could achieve this. However, if you rewrite the essay with a more realistic objective, I will reconsider your grade."

The boy went home and thought for a long time. He even asked his father what he should do. His father responded, "Look, son, you have to decide for yourself. It's an important decision, and I can't make it for you."

After a week of consideration, the boy handed in the same essay without any changes, telling his professor, "You can keep your bad grade. I'm going to keep my dream!"

Many years passed. One day, the teacher, now on the brink of retirement, took a group of thirty children to visit a famous horse stud that bred some of the most spectacular horses in the country. He was amazed when upon meeting the owner, he realized it was the same boy to whom he had given an F!

Upon leaving, the teacher told the owner of the stud, "When I was your teacher many years ago, I was a dream stealer. For years I stole dreams from children. Luckily, you managed to hold on to yours."

The intellect says, "You'll never own a horse stud! Where will you get the money? You're wasting your time on an impossible dream. Be more realistic!"

Love-consciousness works differently. It comes from the heart. Instead of becoming bogged down in thought, it trusts. It trusts the heart.

Who told you that you couldn't realize your dreams? Maybe it was your father or your mother. Or maybe it was your schoolteacher, as it was for the boy in the story.

As you begin practicing the facets I am sharing with you, you will find that the limiting beliefs that have governed your past begin to fall away without any effort on your part. You will find yourself living from love-consciousness instead of from conditioned thoughts and emotions.

You will begin to live your dreams.

The Keys to Abundance

When we use the first facet, we are embracing the fullness of the present moment. Ironically, when we start to experience this inner completion and no longer feel our previous desires, we start to create what we have always wanted in our lives. Our surroundings begin to mirror our inner fulfillment, and everything flows toward us in abundance—loving relationships, material wealth, career opportunities, better health. Every area of life grows and matures as our experience of union expands.

Remember to think the facet: Praise love for this moment in its perfection.

> (Attention: deep in the heart)

Love-consciousness is the most magnetic experience in the universe—it attracts everything to it automatically, from a place of innocence. Instead of limiting our dreams to a fixed idea of what we need in order to be happy, as we become conscious of union, we open ourselves up to the excitement of unpredictability, safe in the knowledge that the universe will provide us with magic that far exceeds the limits of our imagination. We embrace our projects and goals with joyful passion but without the anxiety and obsessive impatience that previously fueled our desires. When we are complete within ourselves, we can truly enjoy all the bounty of the universe, without the fear of loss that used to lurk beneath the surface.

Focus on what you want, but then let it go. Use the facets to embrace the magic of the now, rejoicing in what you have, and your dreams will become a reality. Then when they do, they will just add to your joy, instead of being the conditions upon which your happiness depends.

Beyond Analysis

In modern society, we have learned to analyze everything. From our thoughts and emotions to our actions and decisions, the intellect sifts through our life experiences with meticulous and often obsessive repetition, mulling endlessly over the circumstances we find ourselves in. But this constant analysis, when it has become a compulsive habit, only serves as a distraction, drawing our attention away from the joy that is present in each moment. When you are unifying, negative or mundane thoughts, emotions, and sensations may arise, but you need not analyze them. These experiences are the old habits that are falling away as we elevate our consciousness. Just be happy they're leaving, and return to the facet.

The intellect loves to dissect the human experience, but love-consciousness is different—it just witnesses, without expectation. When you are unifying, your experience will change constantly—there will be thoughts; there will be emotions. Just allow everything to pass through; let it shift and move as the seasons do throughout the year.

Don't start thinking, "Why is it raining today when it's midsummer?" It's raining because it is, and it's perfect that it rains; every day needn't be sunny. If there's a heat wave in the middle of winter, that's perfect too. It just is. Approach your experiences as you do the weather: embrace them in every moment—feel them one hundred percent. Don't get hooked in the *whys, what-fors,* and *how-comes.* Every day will be different. Embrace the changes and say, "I feel sad in this moment. That's just fine." Or, "I'm so happy right now. Fantastic." Whatever happens naturally is perfect.

The mind will always try to analyze, to understand and size up every situation, because it so desperately needs to keep itself entertained. "Am I using the facets properly? Am I letting my thoughts affect me too much? I don't think I'm progressing fast enough.... Oh no, I'm not growing spiritually at all! Everyone else is growing faster than me! Look how much they've all grown!" These are just the games of the mind. Don't get hooked into such thoughts. As soon as you do, they become an attachment. If you just watch them pass, without taking them seriously, they will not cause you any suffering.

We are so attached to our thoughts. We think we *are* our thoughts, but we're not. We think our thoughts are real, but if you watch them, you will see how contradictory they are.

Our thoughts change constantly. The mind dances incessantly from one extreme to another, taking one side, then the other, then both. There is no stability in our thoughts. Freedom comes when you learn to just watch them pass.

We are always growing; we are always moving forward. Whether you can see that or not, even if you think you're worse off than you have ever been in your life, when you use the facets you are always moving toward greater awareness. Sometimes situations or habits in your life will seem to get worse, but that is just your universe opening your eyes to a place where you can cast off your attachments and become more whole and free.

When your inner experience starts to grow, you start to see yourself and your limiting beliefs more clearly. You start to see, "Ah! I fall into that trap over and over again!" But it's not about trying to calculate or comprehend. If you are supposed to understand something, it will become very clear to you. The key is just to feel and to be innocent. Don't analyze—the surest way to slow down the process is by intellectualizing everything.

A philosopher had been pondering God's existence for years, trying to understand the divine. He traveled the world, discussing in depth with theologians, priests, ministers, rabbis—anyone who he thought might have a clearer understanding of the Almighty. One day he was walking down the beach, lost in thought, trying to understand God in all His complexity. He came across a young boy digging a hole in the sand. The boy piqued his curiosity—he wondered why on earth he was digging such a deep hole. The boy dug and dug and dug, until he had made a huge pit. Then he ran to the ocean, collected some water in his hands, and ran back to pour it into the hole.

Finally it was too much for the philosopher. He went up to the boy and asked, "Why are you taking handfuls of the ocean and putting them into that hole?"

"I'm doing the same thing you're doing," the boy replied. "I'm trying to fit the ocean in a hole, just as you are trying to fit God inside your head!"

This is what we try to do: we try to take union and understand it within the confines of duality, but it's impossible. The quicker you let go of the need to understand, and open yourself up to receive your true essence, the quicker you will find the answers, because they will come from your heart, they will come from your nature, they will come from within.

Living from the Heart

The heart sees beyond the comparisons and judgments of the mind. It is able to embrace everything in its perfection, exactly as it is. Such a level of acceptance is hard for the intellect to grasp because it transcends logical thought.

To perceive from love-consciousness is the opposite of perceiving from the intellect. The intellect perceives duality, while love perceives union. The intellect perceives good and bad, right and wrong, whereas love accepts and embraces everything.

I want to talk about perfection for a moment. We hold an idealized notion of what perfection is, as if it were something far off and unattainable, a saintlike ideal achieved only by the certain few. This makes perfection a seemingly unreachable goal toward which we must strive, but perfection is nothing like this.

Perfection is unconditional love. It involves giving with no strings attached, living without judgment, and perceiving beauty in everything. It has nothing to do with moralistic ideals.

To be perfect, all that is required is to accept ourselves *in this moment.* There are *no* preconditions to feeling fully accepted—we embrace ourselves as we are. *Praise love for this moment in its perfection.*

Every time you think this facet, you are choosing union, freedom, love. Think it every time you remember to. You will soon realize that it is always much more productive to think a facet than the countless other contradictory thoughts that jostle constantly for your attention. Let's think it again now:

Praise love for this moment in its perfection.

Remember to gently put your attention deep in your heart as you are thinking the phrase. Don't forget to think the facet while you continue reading, and indeed, in as many moments of your life as possible. This teaching is not about intellectual understanding; it is about experiencing union. It is through practice that we make this experience permanent.

Discovering Perfection

How we perceive the world around us reflects our inner being; the external mirrors the internal. For example, when you feel full of love, your world reflects this love. Your partner, your friends, and your activities mirror the love. Yet if you feel empty inside, nothing on the outside is able to satisfy you.

Perfection is about seeing with the eyes of the heart—seeing with nothing but an overwhelming and unconditional love, no matter how the external circumstances of a situation may appear. When people see in this way, it transforms the whole of life into a beautiful experience. This is because fulfillment, peace, joy, and love have nothing to do with our physical circumstances. They are inner states, to be entered into, not goals to be reached.

The city council of Montevideo in Uruguay became acquainted with the Isha System and invited me to offer a community service to over three hundred disabled people. The event had official support and also received sponsorship from a national bus company to bring individuals from all over the country. They arrived in wheelchairs, some with Down syndrome,

36

others with autism, some blind, others deaf. It was an honor to be able to share the Isha System with such a group of people because they were so appreciative of being able to participate in the event.

> *Remember to think the facet...*

One of the participants was born without arms or legs. To most of us, this would be a tremendous disadvantage. Was this woman limited by her disability? No. When I met her, she had just obtained her law degree and was excited about entering into practice.

This woman's passion and joyful presence moved me deeply. She radiated a happiness I have not seen in many people. Clearly, she knew a freedom that is rare in the world. Her heart was focused on the beauty of each moment, and she derived great joy from her creativity. I was so moved by how present she was that I asked her, "Do you know that you are perfect exactly as you are?"

She looked at me with a smile big enough to fill the whole auditorium. "Yes, Isha, I do know that I am perfect exactly as I am," she responded. Tears filled my eyes.

It may seem strange to you that someone with what we perceive as such a severe disability could see perfection in herself, but I have found that when we view life through the lens of love-consciousness, there is perfection in everything. To be among people who were experiencing this perfection despite their seeming disadvantages was an inspiring experience. It was so clear to me that there was nothing wrong with any of them! In what most people would dismiss as striking imperfection, there was in fact a wonderful perfection.

What we focus on grows. When we focus on love, we become more loving. When we focus on fear, we become more fearful. Similarly, if we focus on our limitations, we become more limited, and when we perceive things as somehow "wrong," they will never appear to be right.

Praise love for this moment in its perfection invites us to see reality so much more deeply than we have ever imagined. It invites us to see from the perspective of union, in which there is nothing but love. It asks us to allow this love to flow into every aspect of our lives.

Simply by practicing this facet, the love begins to manifest, without us having to do anything. The love is *who we are,* and the facet simply unlocks it.

Chapter 2

The Second Facet

Accepting What Is, Without Judgment

A young man carrying a heavy trunk walked up to the gates of a village. Sitting on a nearby rock was an old man smoking a pipe. "What are the people like in this village?" asked the young man.

"What were the people like in the village you are coming from?" he replied.

"They were very disagreeable people—dishonest thieves, ungrateful and bitter. They were always fighting among themselves and trying to take advantage of others. Gossip and resentment were commonplace among them. That is why I am asking before entering, what are the people like here?"

The old man sighed and said, "I'm afraid that here you will not find much difference. The people here are just like the ones from the village you came from."

"Then I think I shall journey onward to the next village," replied the young man, and he set back off along the road.

"Goodbye," said the old man, and he went back to smoking his pipe.

After a while, another young man came up to the village gates. "What are the people in this village like?" he asked.

"What were the people like in the village you are coming from?" the old man replied.

"My people were very agreeable. They were always willing to help one another, and love and compassion were commonplace among them. One could always find a friend who was willing to listen to one's problems. I was sad to have to leave. What are the people like in this village?"

"Here you will not find much difference. The people in this village are the same as the ones from your hometown. Welcome." The young man entered the village.

Looking Outside Ourselves

As adults, the fear-based rigidity that has replaced our innate innocence holds us in the role of victimhood. Like the first young man in the story, we don't want to take responsibility for our dissatisfaction. It's so much easier to blame the world around us. It's easier to blame the politicians, our parents, the church, pollution, our bosses, and so on. It's so much easier to place the blame outside, because that's what we've done all our lives.

We can support a different political party, we can convert to a new faith, we can move to a new city, we can change our external circumstances ad infinitum, but in reality that will never change anything. The outside is just a mirror of our own discontent.

Because we are plagued by anxiety—many of us almost to the point of panic—we are always in search of relief. We seek out anything that can stop the relentless nagging of our thoughts. Some, looking for love outside themselves, seek relief sexually by having casual sex with an endless parade of people. Others do it by consuming copious quantities of alcohol, doing drugs, or overeating. Maybe working obsessively, seeking achievement, chasing the elusive carrot of success is your form of relief. Or perhaps you go shopping as an escape, are addicted to television, or are glued to the Internet.

I am not suggesting there is anything wrong with any of these activities, but none of them truly fulfills us, and none of them ever will. Fulfillment, peace, joy, and love do not come from outside. The one thing that can fulfill the human heart is love-consciousness, and we have abandoned it. When we are anchored in that experience, we automatically find fulfillment. We discover an internal peace and joy that never change and are ever present, ever calling us home.

Until we embrace love-consciousness, we are totally unconscious of life, unable to see beyond the limits of our tiny intellectual boxes—we think they are who we are. Even when we move into a new environment, we take our little world with us, and nothing changes.

The Loss of Innocence

Have you ever watched children building sand castles on the beach? They are a delight to watch, totally absorbed in what they are doing. They run around filling their buckets and make their castle higher and higher. When it finally stands in all its glory, they wait in excitement for the tide to come in and pull it down. Then they happily start again, building another castle.

Do you think that before they started building, they thought, "Oh no, we shouldn't build here—the tide is going to come in and destroy it!" No, that's not how they think. When the waves come, is there anguish? No. Just the excitement of the next project, a new moment, as they intuitively embrace creation and destruction as natural parts of life.

We were all children once. We all once embraced the unexpected tide rushing in, accepting the destruction of what has come before as a natural part of life, remaining open to the unknown magic that awaited us around every corner. As adults, on the other hand, most of us seek to preserve the walls of our sand castles at all costs, in a vain attempt to protect our achievements and possessions from the unpredictability of the world. But it doesn't matter how rigid those walls are; the tide of life will eventually come in and sweep them all away.

The loss of innocence is one of the greatest tragedies of humanity.

As adults, our perception of the world is so tainted by the suffering we have experienced in the past that we are no longer able to see things afresh or to embrace the beauty of the present moment. This loss of innocence perpetually sucks the magic out of our daily experience of life. We perceive ourselves as fragile, vulnerable. We perceive our humanity as full of flaws and weaknesses, and we try to contain our apparent fragility within a false illusion of control.

> *Think the facet.*

During early childhood, we begin to adopt the fears and constraints of those around us. We become limited, needy, and dependent on the outside for approval and support. We watch our parents, our grandparents, and everyone around us, and we learn the codes of manipulation that we must use in order to receive what we want. We learn what emotions are appropriate, and we learn what responses we'll receive when we exhibit those emotions. In short, we learn what works and what doesn't work in order to get what we desire.

As we grow older, we take these behaviors into the classroom and use them with our peers. We learn when to lie and when to tell the truth. We learn what to hide, what to say, what's appropriate, what's polite, what we should like, who we should vote for; in short, we learn how to please our surrounding environment in order to acquire what we want.

Or we go to the other extreme. We have temper tantrums, dye our hair purple, and become rebellious. If our parents are conservative, we become liberals. We drag home the most inappropriate boyfriends or girlfriends we can find, whom we are sure our family couldn't possibly approve of, and we embrace anything that will give us shock value, being contrary in all areas of our lives in order to receive attention.

So there are usually two types of people: the conformist, or "good" girl or boy, and the rebel, or wild child. But it doesn't matter which of these identities we adopt; we are all screaming out for love and approval from the outside world.

Finding Fullfillment Beyond the Material

There was once a poor man who used to pray to God for a treasure that would make him rich. One night, in a dream, he heard a voice that said, "To-morrow a monk will pass by your home asking for food. He has the treasure you seek. Ask him for it!"

The next day, a monk knocked on his door and asked for something to eat. The man remembered the dream and said, "Last night, a strangely familiar voice spoke to me in a dream. It told me that a monk would be passing through the village at midday and that he carried the treasure I have dreamed of for so long. It told me to ask you for it, so give me the treasure that will make me rich!"

The monk fished into his habit and brought out a brilliant diamond, the biggest in the world. He said, "Is this the treasure you speak of ? I found it in the forest. Here, take it." The man grabbed the stone delightedly and thanked the monk, who after eating his fill, continued on his path.

That night, the man could not sleep for fear of losing his newfound treasure. "This house is not safe: anyone could break in and steal my treasure," he thought. "I can't reinforce it because I have no money. Maybe I should sell the diamond, but in such a poor village, who will have the money to buy it? If I travel to sell it somewhere else, I might get mugged."

The next morning, when he awoke, he hurriedly took the diamond and rushed down the trail the monk had taken. After running for hours, he finally found the monk sitting calmly beneath a tree, contemplating nature with an expression of perfect peace.

"I have come to bring you back your diamond," panted the man. *"I have realized that this is not the treasure I seek. What I truly need is the diamond you have within that allows you to detach, without suffering, from such a valuable jewel."*

The man in this story saw in the monk something much more valuable than a diamond. He saw nonattachment and inner fulfillment. When we experience inner completion, we let go of our ideas about what we need in order to be happy. When we stop believing in the intellect's notions of how things are supposed to look, we rediscover the magic of the unknown. Then we find ourselves standing in a room without walls, with our hearts open to receive the abundance of the universe. Finally, we have the greatest treasure of all: freedom from fear, and the innocence to perceive the perfection in everything.

Embracing the Human Experience

As adults, we spend the majority of our time judging and calculating what's wrong with our exterior. We have ideas of how people need to behave, ideas of how we need to behave—so many rules and regulations that we spend the majority of our time struggling to try to function within our social experience. We are always comparing and categorizing everything and everyone around us, always trying to box ourselves into an "ideal" way of being.

We have learned to blame our human experience as the source of our own discontent. We believe there is something fundamentally wrong with it.

We have learned to judge our thoughts, feelings, and emotions. We have learned to judge our peers and friends, our parents and children, our political and religious leaders. Our financial situation, the state of the environment, certain ethnic groups, our sexual preferences—there are so many aspects of our human experience that we have learned to judge that it would be quicker to list the ones we *haven't.*

And let's not forget the judgments we have of our bodies. Modern society has an ever-increasing obsession with youth and physical beauty. As we fight against the scale, the wrinkles, the gray hair, we are fighting against the illusion of time.

The second facet helps us rise above these judgments and complaints of the intellect to embrace the world around us with innocent, joyful acceptance.

From the perception of love-consciousness, there is nothing wrong. The present moment vibrates in unity—there is no duality when we are anchored in the here and now. When we experience love-consciousness, we realize that everything is perfect exactly as it is.

Make no mistake: this does not mean we shouldn't want to improve our situations and grow as people. Evolution is the nature of life, and everything is always moving forward; but if we choose to embrace the beauty of what is happening right now, instead of focusing on what we perceive as wrong, love grows, instead of fear. In doing that, we become increasingly empowered to make positive changes in our lives. When we bring ourselves ever deeper into love-consciousness, our external circumstances become ever more enriching and fulfilling.

The Second Facet

In the second facet, we use the emotion of gratitude, which stems naturally from the uplifting qualities of praise.

Thank love for my human experience in its perfection.

As you are thinking the last part of the phrase, *in its perfection,* gently bring your attention deep into your heart. Let's think this second facet, without concentrating or forcing in any way, as we continue.

Please do not confuse this phrase with passivity. Embracing things as they are is not being passive at all. We are simply choosing to focus on the love in this moment, embracing life in this moment. We are doing something different, changing our inner attitude, to focus on love. Then our surroundings will reflect that love back to us.

Here's how to practice the second facet:

1. Sit comfortably and close your eyes. Allow any thoughts that come to mind to pass. Remember, whatever thoughts come naturally are perfect.

2. Think the second facet: *Thank love for my human experience in its perfection.* Think it without any effort, the same way you might think any other thought.

3. As you think the last part of the phrase, *in its perfection,* bring your attention deep into your heart.

4. After thinking the facet, leave a space. After a few moments, repeat the thought and again leave a space.

5. Continue in this way for about twenty minutes. You can glance at your watch or a clock to check the time.

How did you feel while practicing this facet? Maybe you had a deeper experience than you did with the first facet, or maybe it was more superficial. No matter what we feel when we unify, we are healing, so it is best to unify without expectations of any kind.

From this point forward, you can think either of the first two facets with your eyes open, in whatever order they naturally arise in. If one comes more than the other, that is fine. When you unify with your eyes closed, however, divide each session between the two facets—ten minutes with the first facet, and ten minutes with the second facet.

Falling in Love with Life

Most of us dream of an ideal world. We want our lives to be free of pain. We want the nations to be at peace. We want an end to famine. We want to abolish racial prejudice, gender discrimination, and poverty. A so-called perfect world is the ideal for most humans.

We will create such a world, but not through the mind.

As we elevate love-consciousness, the separations we perceive in the world fall away. We increasingly focus on the inherent unity of everything. We embrace the perfection of this moment. We fall in love with life. In the wake of full acceptance come all the changes that are needed, because only love can birth our dreams.

As I embrace every aspect of myself, the judgments I have made about myself dissolve. And the more I am at home with myself, the more I become at home in the world. My external world becomes a reflection of how I perceive myself. I stop noticing all its divisions, separations, and inadequacies. Instead, I see its glory. I no longer see good and bad or right and wrong but see everything as just how it is meant to be.

An experience I had in Santiago, Chile, demonstrates how our perception changes through the experience of love-consciousness. I was walking down a busy street looking for a shoeshine boy. On a windy corner, I spotted one. As I drew closer, I was surprised to recognize him as a student of mine. It turned out that this young man had carefully saved every penny he made from his shoe shining in order to come and learn the Isha System.

We got into a conversation about how the facets were changing his life. He related how, as he practiced them, he found himself becoming increasingly happy.

This young man had a deformed hand, which he usually kept hidden, but now he showed it to me with pride. "I used to hide my hand and just work with the other one," he said. "But since I learned the System, I have increasingly been loving this hand. So I bring it out into the open. I even use it to polish shoes! Thanks to the System, I can now work with *both* hands."

"That's not all," he went on, his grin broadening, his eyes alight with excitement. "Something even better has happened. I was on my bike and I got hit by a bus!" Now this really made me pause. I mean, how could anyone be excited about being hit by a bus?

"When the bus hit me," he continued enthusiastically, "I fell to the ground and cut my head open. There was a lot of blood. Normally I would have passed out because I am afraid of blood, but I started unifying, and I didn't pass out!"

This loving soul had discovered an amazing acceptance of himself and the things that happen to him. I was touched by the beauty, innocence, and positivity of his newfound perception.

Destroying the Illusion of Separation

In this world of duality, we all feel different from one another. We meet thousands of people, from many races, with varying physical conditions, of different ages, contrasting religions, and opposing political beliefs, philosophies, convictions, and ideals. The complex diversity of the world we live in is seemingly endless—from our intellectual opinions to the sizes of our bank accounts, from our physical appearances to our cultural traditions. We perceive separation everywhere, in a world of extreme contrast and variance, a world of untold possibilities.

Within this experience of separation, we search endlessly for union. We strive to heal the planet, we create programs for conflict resolution, we march for peace, trying desperately to get humanity to see beyond its differences and live in harmony.

We do this in our personal lives too, putting all our energy into trying to create balance in our surroundings. We search for the perfect partner, but when we think we have finally found our soul mate, we try to change and control them so they will fit into our ideal. We search for groups of people who will make us feel accepted by supporting us in our convictions, our opinions, our beliefs. We join churches, political parties, self-help groups, and corporations in our search to heal the separation in our surroundings, to find the place where we belong.

But in this search, we are vainly trying to accommodate the beliefs and opinions of the intellect. When someone disagrees with how we perceive the world, we avoid him or her. We try to surround ourselves with people who confirm our convictions, who support us in our ideas, however negative or fear-based those ideas may be. Like butterflies, we flit from one experience to another, our minds never fully satisfied, on an endless quest to find what feels like home.

The mind will never feel satisfied. Wherever it goes, it will find disagreement. Even within groups that appear to be united, there is separation—religions branch off into countless factions; political parties disagree among themselves; football teams argue about tactics; even the Beatles split up. Everywhere we look, there is separation, divergence, duality.

Remember to think the facets when you drive.

So we continue on our search, rejecting other groups as wrong. Or we fanaticize about the particular perspective of our chosen organization or religion, in our desperate need to convince ourselves and the world that we are right. In our quest for union, in reality we are creating more separation, as our prejudices and opinions distance us further from the rest of humanity, instead of bringing us together in love.

The irony is, we are all exactly the same. It is only our perception that is different. It doesn't matter where you go in the world; everyone is looking for love. It could be the guerrilla in the jungles of Colombia torturing someone or a missionary preaching in India, helping the poor. We are all looking for love. We are all looking to come back home.

Whether we're in Buckingham Palace playing the role of a princess, or we're a crack junkie in Harlem holding a knife to someone's throat, we have all suffered abandonment of self. We have all suffered self-abuse, and we all perceive ourselves as unworthy of love, with a multitude of masks covering the things we consider sins.

Everyone is playing their part in this grand opera called life, like the actors on a stage—each with their own role to play. Some are knights in shining armor, others mysterious villains, but the truth—our essence, our greatness—is infinitely the love. Everyone everywhere can choose to be that.

Love-consciousness is inspired by people's hearts. It admires greatness, irrespective of the views of the individual. It is touched by the passion of visionaries from totally different, sometimes directly opposing, walks of life. They may come from competing political parties. They may have totally incompatible belief systems. It's not their politics it admires, or their point of view—it's the truth of their hearts.

That's what life is all about. It's about being true to your heart. It's not about being right or wrong. If you vote for the left, the right are going to say you're wrong. If you vote for the right, the left are going to say you're wrong. And if you don't vote, they will both say you're wrong! There will always be some who agree with you and many who don't.

Christians think Jesus is great, but there are millions of other people who don't think so. Does that mean he wasn't great, just because many people disagree? No—he was great. He embodied pure consciousness; he taught tolerance and unconditional love. But many people have taken those teachings and used them to separate themselves from others. What would Jesus think about that?

World Peace through the Union of Love

The concept of world peace, the vision of a world united in love, is beyond the intellect. Its very nature is beyond all belief systems, because belief systems are based in difference of opinion. The initiative for world peace, then, must be based in something much bigger, something of much greater importance, something permanent; it must be based in unconditional love. Unconditional love is the only thing we all have in common; it is the one thing that unites us. When we anchor in unconditional love, the power of the intellect—its separation and ideas—becomes like a distant echo. Our differences are no longer important. They are just threads of different hues, adding color to the rich tapestry of life. United in love-consciousness, we meld as one, coming back to the experience of pure, unconditional love in everything—within the contrasts of duality, within the illusion of separation.

When our judgments fall, we perceive beauty in the duality. We are no longer trying frantically to change it. Ironically, when this happens, the things that we judge as bad—violence, rape, starvation, poverty, cruelty, and so on—start to fall away naturally; as consciousness elevates, the things such as these that vibrate on a low frequency start to remove themselves from our human experience and the world around us.

When people are complete within themselves, they stop needing to protect, control, or grasp because the nature of love, the nature of love-consciousness, is to give to every aspect of itself. Love perceives itself in everything. It perceives no scarcity or lack. In love, a new perception is born, a new vision for life.

Once there was a young crocodile. He was lying on a log in a river, basking in the sun. He had a very serious look on his face—it's a very intense business, being a crocodile! Crocodiles have a long history to live up to—as carnivorous predators, cold-blooded assassins, and direct descendants of the dinosaurs. This crocodile was pondering his great responsibility when all of a sudden, a beautiful red butterfly landed on his nose.

At first, he was indignant. Couldn't she see that he was deep in thought, that he was contemplating serious matters? But she seemed oblivious, and every time he breathed, she would float up in the air and then gently return, caressing his nose with her velvet-soft wings. Then he'd breathe again, and up she'd go, and then gently she'd come back.

This became like a meditation for the crocodile, and the energy changed completely. He was mesmerized by the butterfly's beauty and softness, and the energy of love began to grow between them. A happiness spread through his being. He was no longer a crocodile, and she was no longer a butterfly. They were one, in the union of love.

When humanity puts away its differences and comes back to the perfection of union, we will experience harmony and peace on this planet. But first, it must begin with our own hearts.

The ideal world is found within. There is nothing to change outside—we need only to heal ourselves.

True Vision

We create the feeling of victimhood in many areas of our lives. Maybe our color seems to be working against us, or our gender, or our creed. Or perhaps it is simply our personal preferences that cause us to stand out from the crowd so that we find ourselves being picked on or passed over in some way.

The norms of society change depending where we are born. In some societies, the opportunities open to people seem limitless. In others, there appear to be all kinds of restrictions. Our religion or political system may appear to be huge barriers to becoming who we wish to be. But true greatness, which flows from love-consciousness, is never thwarted by external circumstances. It has no limits and pushes all boundaries to achieve what it desires.

I was able to appreciate this when meeting a group of blind people who came to learn the Isha System. Most of us would view blindness as just about the worst thing that could happen to a person. How could one be fulfilled and happy if one were blind? But many who are blind "see" much more clearly than those of us who have the gift of eyesight. I learned from speaking with the group at the seminar that their blindness opened them to an experience of the other senses that far surpasses what most of us ever enjoy. Blind people can perceive with crystal clarity the perfection of a robin's trill. Their sense of smell can distinguish the essences of a hundred delicate flowers. Lucky them. *Poor us!*

We are blinded by how things look on the surface, convinced that our conditioned perceptions of ourselves and our world are real. Because our thoughts do not allow us to see beyond the constraints of duality, we don't realize that so much of what we *think* we see is illusion.

Thank love for my human experience in its perfection.

Even those who consider themselves to be conscious and aware will discover a new depth to their perception when they become truly present.

When we see with the heart, we encounter a world of beauty we did not know existed.

The Unity That Lies Beyond Diversity

On the peaks of the Andes, water turns into snow. It changes form, but it's still water. Then it changes again and becomes a glacier, a river of ice. Then the lake and the sun seduce the glacier and it starts to melt and unite with the river. It too is incredibly beautiful, the bluest blue you have ever seen. Yet it is still water.

Water changes form millions upon millions of times. In each of its forms, it's splendid—but it is still water; it never ceases to be water. Lapping on the seashore, it is gentle, refreshing, comforting. In a tsunami, it can be consuming and destructive. As billowing clouds, it casts shadows across the landscape, then falls as rain, breathing new life into the earth below. Drunk from a spring, it can be healing and nourishing. Yet you can also drown in it, as it steals your last breath.

Love is like this too. As your consciousness expands, you realize that love is *all* there is. Everything in the universe is a manifestation of this love. The burning furnace at the core of the sun, and the warmth of sunshine on your face—it's all an expression of love.

Once you recognize that there is only love, you see the magic and wonder of everything. You see the love in people's anger, the love in their jealousy, the love even in their hatred. No matter what emotions they express, you recognize that all of it is nothing other than love seeking to break through.

Tears can be running down your face because you think you're suffering. It's still love. Or you can be mesmerized by the eyes of a lover, and the tears will still be falling. They are still water, and it's still the love. It never, ever leaves. It's always there.

When you are anchored in love-consciousness, love is all you see, and in all its forms, it is perfect.

Chapter 3

The Third Facet

Loving Oneself

Once there was a donkey who lived on a Colombian coffee farm. He worked hard every day, helping the farmer carry his produce. One day the donkey slipped on a loose stone and fell into a deep pit. The farmer and his workers gathered around the hole and were surprised to see that the donkey had survived the fall. However, the pit was so deep and its sides were so steep and unstable that none of the men dared climb in to save him. They decided to leave him there to die.

As they walked away, the donkey's frantic braying was too much for them to bear, and they decided to end his misery. They began throwing earth into the pit to bury him. When the donkey saw the earth falling in on top of him, he shuffled about a little, stamping it into the ground. The farmers continued to shovel, and the donkey continued stamping the earth down beneath him. Bit by bit, the earth beneath the donkey's hooves began piling up, inching him closer and closer to the mouth of the pit. After a while, the farmer and his men realized what the clever little donkey was doing, and they began shoveling faster and faster—now not to bury him but to help him rise up and out of the hole. As the earth piled up, filling the hole, the donkey rose to the surface.

Whether we suffer depends not on our surroundings but on our perception. The donkey chose to embrace what was happening and use what appeared to be a cruel act of destruction in order to free himself from the pit. It is a choice we make in every moment. What are you choosing in this moment?

We have so many ideas of how things need to look, and we suffer whenever things are not the way we think they should be. We are so attached to receiving the approval and support of everyone around us, so dependent on the way they behave, that when *they* change, *we* suffer.

If you are desperate for love from the outside world, give it to yourself. If you experience anxiety or neediness in any of your personal relationships—or perhaps because you *lack* a particular kind of relation-ship—or if you need someone to change in order to feel happy, you need to go inward and love yourself. Speak your truth, but then come back to yourself, always. It's never about changing the outside.

Until we take responsibility for our own happiness—un-til we realize that we and we alone are accountable for our satisfaction, we will remain dissatisfied.

In every moment, you have the power to reinvent yourself. You can choose to be whatever you want to be. That's the wonderful thing about being human—we have a choice, and we can change. We can change to be more love, more freedom, to let go of our limitations, to start living in the moment—to start new habits that don't cause us to suffer.

True consciousness takes responsibility. It doesn't perceive the world as something separate from itself. It takes responsibility because it knows that it is the world.

If I'm always criticizing myself, if I'm always comparing and complaining, if I'm not just being the brilliance of who I am, then who is responsible? I am. Everyone is unique and perfect and brilliant, but you have to find that brilliance by polishing your facets. It's your choice, no one else's. "I choose to be the greatness of who I am, and I can do that. I can't be someone else—I can be the greatness of who I am, and that's great enough." In fact, it's the greatest thing there is, because once you find that, there's no comparison, no jealousy, no insecurity; there's just love. Then you can extend that to every part of your creation, and you can surrender and embrace your world with joy. You'll find joy, because you're not comparing; you're just enjoying the variance of your beautiful creation.

A Perfect World

As the vibration of love rises in all of humanity, our ideal world will become a global reality. But it will come about through an internal change—through seeing with different eyes. It will come about as we embrace the perfection that is always present—the perfection of consciousness, of love.

Many of us aspire to unconditional love. We know it's the ideal way to live, and we try to mimic it. We put on an act, behaving as we imagine an unconditionally loving person ought to behave.

But how can we truly love another if we cannot love ourselves? How can we embrace others exactly as they are if we are incapable of accepting ourselves exactly as we are?

To be pure love, you have to be pure love. You cannot copy how pure love is meant to look. You cannot duplicate what you see another doing; that is nothing more than a trick of the intellect.

When we try to love others without loving ourselves, we abandon ourselves, putting other people's happiness before our own. We compromise our own being, and this can only lead to resentment—quite the opposite of what we are aspiring to be.

How do you become unconditionally loving? You embrace your perfection in this very moment. You accept that there is nothing wrong with you—that you are perfect exactly as you are.

We are *perfectly human,* which is what we are *meant* to be.

When we come to love ourselves unconditionally, we can truly love everyone else unconditionally. This is because when we find the perfection within ourselves through the light of unconditional love, we perceive perfection in everything.

All these ideas may be quite revolutionary to you, and you may find them difficult to understand, but if you keep doing the same things you have always done, you will continue to receive the same results. If, on the other hand, you wish to experience change, you need to do something different. You do not need to understand at this point—just practice the facets. As they do their work, everything that holds you back from the experience of love-consciousness, keeping you from perceiving perfection in yourself and in your surroundings, will begin to fall away.

Learning to Love Yourself

Within nature, there is an instinctive calling to protect and separate. In the thousands of hectares of pristine

South American pampas, stallions graze with their herds of mares. Each stallion will protect his mares at all costs—when the younger colts start to mature, the stallions cast them out from the herd so they can't get near the mares. The stallions will fight to the death to protect what is theirs, their harem. The only way they will give up their mares is if another, more powerful stallion conquers them.

Sadly, we humans emulate this instinctive animal behavior. We're always defending our belief systems, our herds, our ideals—what we perceive to be ours—and in some cases we'll even die in defense of those things. Why? Because we are still trapped within the illusion of separation.

We have forgotten the fact that we are all one, that there is no lack, nothing to protect. The reason we feel this scarcity, this separation is because we do not feel complete within ourselves. We do not love ourselves.

People used to say to me, "You need to love yourself."

"That's a good idea!" I would reply. "How?" No one seemed to have an answer to that.

Many of us think that loving ourselves means buying a new sports car. Then we're loving ourselves! Or a bigger house. Then we're loving ourselves even more!

Or finding a new partner. We are always changing our surroundings (including the people that surround us), thinking that in doing so, we are giving to ourselves, but nothing ever seems to be enough. We always want something more. Finally we have to realize that it isn't working.

What about our bodies? How do you feel about your body? All of our bodies are different. Yet all of us, at least at some time in our lives, have learned to judge our body as unattractive or imperfect. Maybe you have wanted to be taller, shorter, thinner, stronger, younger. Maybe you have wished you could change certain bits and pieces—your hair color or receding hairline, the shape of your hips, the size of your biceps or breasts. The negative beliefs we have about our bodies come from the matrix of the intellect; they are a product of our conditioning.

When I was younger, no matter how fit I was, I was always focused on what was wrong with my body. But ultimately I realized I just had to change myself. I had to learn to love myself.

What is love of self? It means being real and accepting every aspect of ourselves. We are having a human experience, in a unique human body. We are not having an idealistic, saintly experience. We are *human.* We get angry, we feel sad, we love, we are selfish, we are generous. We are everything. We lie, we hide—we do *everything.* We are human!

We all have parts of ourselves that we judge. We all have secrets, things we think we did wrong that we reproach ourselves for. All these things have been created through our own self-abandonment. But we must embrace them all if we want to experience love of self.

> *Think a facet whenever you feel nervous or impatient.*

This means we accept the fact that many of our actions are based in fear and are just habitual, unconscious reactions. It means we start to see that there is nothing wrong with those actions, that they are just some of the vibrant colors that form the landscape of the human experience. They are the springboard from which the truth of who we are can take flight.

The Third Facet

In the third facet, we are going to create a profound truth that will bring us back to love of self. This thought will lead us to embrace ourselves in our perfection, to recognize that we can recreate ourselves afresh in every moment.

Love creates me in my perfection.

Here's how to practice the third facet:

1. Sit comfortably and close your eyes. Remember, any thoughts that come are perfect—don't avoid them.

2. Think, *Love creates me in my perfection.* Remember to think it just as you would any other thought, without forcing or straining.

3. At the same time that you think this thought, put your attention deep in the heart.

4. After thinking the facet, leave a space. After a few moments, repeat the thought and again leave a space.

5. Continue in this way for about twenty minutes. You can glance at your watch or a clock to check the time.

Now that you have three facets, use them for equal amounts of time when you unify with your eyes closed. For example, if you are going to unify for half an hour, start with ten minutes of the first facet, then spend ten minutes on the second, and end with ten minutes of the third. You can glance at your watch to check the time.

When you unify with your eyes open, you can think whichever facet comes to mind in any given moment.

The Illusion of Romantic Love

When we are experiencing love-consciousness, we are complete within ourselves. We are no longer waiting for someone on the outside to fulfill us.

The thrill of romance is something many of us seek tirelessly—the pursuit, the candlelit dinners, the flowers, the songs, all the theatrics. But in reality, we are seeking distraction: the excitement and fantasy are just ways of avoiding the lack of love we feel within ourselves.

With love-consciousness, this need to distract ourselves falls away. All the expectations we place on the outside and on our partners—all the reasons we feel unfulfilled within our relationships—just vanish, because we have created a relationship with ourselves. It is based in true love. It isn't like romantic love. It is whole and it is complete.

Once you have discovered love of self, romance might appear in your life as an added bonus, but it will no longer be a requirement for your contentment.

In a recent conversation, a friend of mine told me that she hadn't seen a certain man for nine months.

She hadn't thought about him. He'd never even crossed her mind. Then she received a phone call from him, and her mind instantly hooked her into the feeling of longing, of how much she missed him and how much she needed him. She started to feel what she called "the presence of the absence." This thought made her start to suffer.

This is our automatic, habitual response to romantic love—neediness, suffering, and idealized memories of how wonderful everything was. The truth is, romantic love seldom has anything to do with reality. It is a fantasy that we create in our minds to entertain ourselves, so that we can feel the adrenaline, the anguish, the elation, the attraction, and the desire. The good news is that my friend realized this. She saw how she had instantly fallen back into a pattern more ancient than the first tango and so ingrained in her being that it was her instant response.

This reminds me of a scene on the children's TV program *Sesame Street* with Bert and Ernie. Bert is very late coming home, and Ernie wonders where he is. Ernie starts to imagine what might have happened to him. Maybe he met his friend Fred and they started talking about Ernie and saying terrible things about him. Ernie continues thinking about all the things they might be saying about him. He thinks that they don't like to spend time with Ernie because he is no fun, that they think he is selfish and cheap with his money and isn't a very good friend. Ernie gets so upset imagining everything that they might be talking about that when Bert finally gets home, Ernie screams at him, "How could you say all those terrible things about me to Fred?" Bert replies, "I never saw Fred. What are you talking about? I was stuck in traffic."

Why do we do this? Why do we choose to fall into a place of discontent so quickly? As we become more conscious of self, we realize we do it because we are addicted to suffering.

Our Addiction to Suffering

There is comfort in suffering, in being a victim, because we don't have to take responsibility; it's much easier to blame someone else for our own discontent.

I used to be totally addicted to suffering. I was always trying to save everyone around me, because it made me feel important—I could support the whole world! Then I felt like a victim of the people I was trying to save because I gave and gave and gave, and I ended up feeling unappreciated. What I didn't realize was that this was a position that I enjoyed—I enjoyed feeling like a victim to the world.

Our addiction to suffering reaches such an extent that even when everything seems to be going perfectly, we find a reason to suffer. Everything is going far too well! It's too good to be true. We test it because we are convinced that it's not real—"If I do this, I wonder if she will still love me. Aha, I knew it! My suspicions were correct!"

Our discontent comes from the matrix of the intellect—judging, comparing, analyzing. We hook into the doubts of the mind and feel trapped by the situations in our lives. The fears of the mind pull us into this place of disenchantment.

How do we break the addiction to suffering? By embracing the perfection of this moment. The mind is always looking for an excuse to reject the present moment, always looking for what is wrong in our lives. This is what suffering is—the feeling that there is something wrong, a reason why we cannot experience absolute fulfillment here and now. If you stop flailing around trying to change everything and come back to the innocence, you will break this addiction. Innocence embraces everything with joy—it has no expectations or ideas of how things need to look.

Remember to think a facet whenever you are in a confrontational situation.

Unconditional Relationships

Some people lose themselves completely in their relationships, and the only thing they care about is their partner. They are not focused on loving themselves, and they don't speak their truth—they compromise so as not to annoy their partner, and in doing so, they lose all their power. Does that serve? No, it doesn't serve their growth at all. But to grow with another person in a relationship, together as individuals, is something very magical.

In order to find love in another, remember that you must first have that experience within yourself, because your partner is a mirror. If there is a lack of love, it will be reflected.

Often in relationships one person is more interested in the relationship than the other. Then sometimes that changes, and the partners swap roles. This is because in most relationships, we are looking for our partners to fill a void within ourselves, and we mirror that need to each other. In the beginning, one partner might appear to be very secure and the other needy and dependent, but this can change with the circumstances. Ultimately, when these dynamics are present, there is no unconditional love of self, and the relationship is based in addiction.

You can grow in a relationship, but only when you are aware of not losing yourself. Then you can have a beautiful partnership based in maturity and love-consciousness, supporting each other in your greatness.

True love in its purest form is unconditional. This is real love. It comes from within and it moves outward. True love gives to every aspect of the self, without need and without compromise. True love comes from a place of innocence. It is conscious love, and it is fulfilled and complete within itself. All the other kinds of love we experience have conditions. They are what we *perceive* as love within the human experience, but they are not expressions of true love. These kinds of love may present themselves as romantic love or as the love of a friend, a business partner, a child, or an animal. But this love has conditions.

The ideal relationship is like a chrysalis, nourishing the growth of each individual so that both can achieve the perfection of their own brilliance, find their wings, and display their true colors. Then both partners mirror more growth and perfection to each other. When they sustain each other in growth, they cannot lose anything that is real. They might endure difficult times together. The seasons may change—there can be harsh winters and bountiful springtimes, but the changing seasons bring each aspect of the self to maturity. The partners support each other through this, and then all that remains is the love.

When we are fully conscious, we are our own perfect partner. When we are so anchored within, so deep in unconditional love, we can be with another person, but it is no longer a need. In that case, the love is focused on more growth, on being more and more love. It's not about trying to complete ourselves with the other person, because we both are complete unto ourselves.

When a child makes a new friend, he doesn't say to his friend, "Now, do you promise me that you'll be my friend forever?" No, he just enjoys the moment. He lives innocently. He plays innocently. He doesn't have a list of expectations and requirements—physical attributes, religious beliefs, sexual preferences, financial stability, willingness to commit, family approval, and so on. He just innocently has a friend who has reached in and enlightened his heart. They have found joy together and they play together.

Conscious Sexuality

A union between two conscious people who love unconditionally is the ultimate sexual expression. It is a deeply nurturing experience, based in mutual growth. The sexual energy in a conscious relationship is very different from what many of us experience because it is based in giving, not in taking. Unconditional love gives. It is complete within itself and finds pleasure in sharing this fullness.

When we do not feel complete within ourselves, sex can become an insatiable need, as we search for physical gratification to try and fill the emptiness we feel inside. Is there anything wrong with casual sex? No, of course not—there is nothing *wrong* with anything—but sex alone will never bring lasting satisfaction.

Sexual repression is deeply ingrained within many aspects of modern society. Many men and women have the deep-seated fear or belief that they are doing something wrong when they have sex. Of course, the underlying belief that there is something bad or impure about sex prohibits the full expression of our sexuality.

As the facets allow this repression to leave, you will find that your sex life becomes more fulfilling. When you anchor in self-love, sex is no longer a compulsive necessity, since you are no longer looking for fulfillment outside yourself.

The facets take you deeper into love-consciousness—when you use them, you are connecting with higher frequencies of love. If you use the facets while making love, you will find that the feeling of pleasure becomes deeper, more intense. Using the facets makes you very present in the moment—instead of making a shopping list or running away with a fantasy in your head, you're *here, now.* That will obviously increase the intensity of your pleasure. Using the third facet while making love is the Isha System's answer to Viagra!

A Game Called Life

Let's play a game. For now, it may seem strange or unrealistic to you, but I am not asking you to believe what I am going to tell you. Remember, it is just a game.

Imagine for a moment that you are God. The creator of totality, the owner of the world. You create this world and can change it at any moment. You have all the power. I want you to imagine with an open heart that everything you believe, everything you see, every idea you have, is ultimately not based in truth. It is just something that you as God have designed from your imagination. You were never born; you will never die. You never came, because you never left. You have always been everything, for eternity. There is nothing to fear, and there is nothing wrong—you are perfect exactly as you are, and the only thing that exists is love.

Imagine that the game you decided to play was to forget that you were God and to have an experience based in duality. Within this human experience, you created the most complex web of separation. Every person and every thing is you, playing a different part. Everyone is creating this grand spectacle for you. It's as if the whole of creation were a huge mirror, reflecting all your loves and hates, your joys and separation.

Imagine that the world is not millions of years old, that it is not this massive, unlimited universe but is instead the tiniest speck of information—information that you had the power to create, and you have the power to change.

You spend your whole life looking for one thing: love. The irony of the human experience is that *that is exactly who you are.* What if we were all one, all God, and the only thing that was real was love?

So how are we going to break free of this perception of separation? How are we going to come back to our true nature? How are we going to experience unconditional love of self and union with the whole of creation? Ultimately there is one answer, and the answer is

Enlightenment.

Destroying the Myths of Enlightenment

We tend to perceive enlightenment as something beyond our human capacity. We believe that enlightenment is for "special" people like Buddha and Jesus. But what if Buddha and Jesus were demonstrating a very real potential, something that was and is attainable for all humans? The experience of love in everything is a reality; it is just that we have forgotten that reality. As you expand your consciousness and new realizations arise, you will see that your heart is continuously yearning for more and more love-consciousness. Ultimately, it yearns to sit in union.

People often think that to presume or even strive for enlightenment would be arrogant. But enlightenment is neither arrogant nor humble; it is just real. It feels no need to hide behind a mask of false modesty or to try to fit into a preconceived idea of how it is supposed to behave. We often compromise our truth by playing small in order to make others feel better about themselves. We don't do what we really want to because we are afraid of losing approval, but enlightenment never compromises its own greatness.

Greatness has the courage to stand alone. Greatness is solitary but never lonely. It is complete within itself. Arrogance, on the other hand, is the abandonment of self. Arrogance is God playing small. Arrogance is God being a victim and not taking responsibility for her creations.

Arrogance is the most magnificent creatures on the planet destroying themselves relentlessly, trying to achieve something that's unachievable outside themselves. Arrogance is the adoption of masks in the form of judgments, political or religious opinions, and false piety to simply fit in and find approval. Arrogance is humans condemning one another for their color, religion, or sexuality.

Remember to think a facet to come back to the present moment.

Enlightenment is love of self. This has nothing to do with arrogance. We have been taught that loving ourselves is selfish, but if I do not know unconditional love of myself, I cannot extend it to the rest of humanity.

Another commonly held misconception is that enlightenment is a state of disconnection from reality. On the contrary, enlightenment anchors you more than ever in life. When you transcend the fears of the mind, you embrace life with freedom and joy. You become more present, not less. This is the glory of enlightenment—you continue to live the human experience while anchored permanently in the vibration of absolute love.

This is also true of our emotions. We often think that enlightenment is a state of emotional inactivity, but in reality, emotions move much more freely as consciousness expands. We feel every emotion fully, without judgment, just as a child feels. As we burst into unconditional love of self, we embrace the spontaneity that is natural to us.

This self-acceptance is inherent in all animals and can be best understood by observing nature. At Puerto Madryn in Argentina, for example, dozens of right whales come to breed in the calm waters surrounding the Valdes Peninsula. It is amazing to get close to such enormous creatures. They are the biggest animals in the world and surely among the most powerful, yet all they do is radiate love. It's incredible. It's all you can feel. They are pure peace, pure love, and yet they are so big. They look at you lazily through the shimmering water as if you're some rare breed of insect, and then down they go again.

The whales come with their babies, and those babies drink two thousand liters of milk a day. So poor Mom spends most of her time nursing. All the baby wants to do is feed—he'd be happy to drink *ten* thousand liters of milk a day. When she gets tired of feeding him, she rolls over onto her back so he can't reach her nipples. The baby starts slapping Mom with his tail in an attempt to make her roll over. It's a relatively powerful thing to have a baby whale slapping you with its tail, but Mom just lies there in perfect peace. She lets him have his little temper tantrum and continues to rest, even when he's getting annoyed. She doesn't judge herself; she doesn't think, "I shouldn't get tired so easily. I'm not giving enough to my children, poor things." Animals never judge themselves. To them everything is perfect.

When the mother has rested, she teaches the baby how to jump out of the water. When Mom jumps, it's magnificent. It's poetry in motion. When the baby tries to copy, he's a disaster! He does big belly flops and isn't impressive at all. But his mother doesn't say, "Oh my God, you're not doing it properly! You're embarrassing me in front of the other whales! I mustn't be a very good teacher..." No. She just keeps leaping, and he keeps practicing, until they are in perfect union, perfect synchrony.

Nature doesn't judge. It's pure love, pure being, perfectly in the moment because it's not thinking all the time. Such is the nature of enlightenment.

Enlightenment is absolute freedom, absolute love of self, union with everything. It means being in joy in every moment for no particular reason instead of constantly waiting for fulfillment in the future. It is life without fear.

My life used to be the opposite of enlightenment. Things had to look a certain way in order for me to be happy. Everything and everyone had to be exactly how I thought they should be, or I could not find peace of mind. I was extremely attached to everything—my country, my ideas, my friends and family, even my dog.

Now I flow with everything. I can find perfection in any situation. I experience joy and freedom everywhere, no matter where I am or whom I'm with. To have that completion is incredible. It's what we search for all our lives. We spend all our energy trying to achieve that experience. We change our external circumstances in a desperate attempt to find that fulfillment—we look for the perfect partner, we relocate, we change careers, or we go on a shopping spree—anything that might appease the relentless discontent of the mind.

We try all these things, but freedom can only come from within. It is an internal experience.

Embrace the magic. We are so lost in our stress that we never notice the magic all around us. We're not present in the moment. We can be in the most beautiful places on Earth, surrounded by spectacular panoramic views, but we can't truly appreciate it—because we are never really there. We are always somewhere else, preoccupied with a future moment or a past regret.

The slightest contact with love-consciousness changes everything in an instant. When you experience that, everything else becomes secondary. Because your heart knows. It never forgets.

When I was a child, my family used to take me on long road trips across Australia. I remember sitting in the back seat looking out the window, captivated by the magnificent landscapes flashing by. I loved to recite the words on the passing road signs in an attempt to impress my mother with my extensive vocabulary.

I enjoyed the drives immensely, unless we came across any dead animals. Australia's animal kingdom is wonderfully diverse. Unfortunately, some of that diversity inevitably becomes nighttime road kill on the highways of the outback. If there were any dead animals on or beside the road, I would always spot them. The sight of anything dead, any beautiful creature, used to terrorize me. It threw me immediately into a shocked, frustrated sadness. I would start to cry, a heavy fog covering my previous enjoyment. This was instant and automatic. I perceived such cruelty—I felt the animals' suffering, even from my childhood innocence. When I grew older, I became equally troubled by the injustices of modern society.

Now I have dedicated my life to elevating consciousness, but I do this from the experience of perfection. I no longer perceive things as wrong or as a reason for me to suffer. I am working to enhance our quality of life in every moment, but I do so from a place of joy, not from a place of pity.

Finding Love in Everything

The perplexities of love are incomprehensible to the human intellect. Love is the greatest force that exists, the only thing that exists, yet we experience it on such a minimal level. As it starts to expand, it encompasses everything until it completely nullifies the experience of separation and suffering.

Suffering has nothing to do with love. Love doesn't know what suffering is. Love is an underlying joy and peace that is present in everything. True love surrenders to each moment. It says yes to what is. Its nature is to give, and it finds an infinite joy in its nature. It gives without expectation and without resentment, because true love, unconditional love, knows that when it gives to others, it is giving to itself.

Love is the mountains. Love is the thunderclouds. Love is the morning rays of the sun playing gently on your face.

Love is the garbage bag that wraps itself around your feet on a windy day.

Love is the partner that you gaze at longingly over a candlelit dinner.

Love is the street thug that holds a knife to your throat as he removes your wallet from your back pocket.

Love is the joy of children playing in the sand, constructing their sand castles, and love is the ocean that tears them down and pulls them back into the sea.

Love is the cancer that sucks away the last breath of your human experience, and love is the painful contractions as you deliver the gift of a newborn baby.

Where can I not find love? There is nowhere I cannot find love. It is the only thing that exists. It's the greatness of who you truly are. It is everything.

This is the freedom we experience with the awakening of love-consciousness. When we love ourselves unconditionally, we perceive our immortality and our enlightenment. We start to love everyone and every-thing around us unconditionally. In the midst of unconditional love, true compassion is born.

Chapter 4

The Fourth Facet

Being One with the Universe

A young boy ran up to his grandfather. "Grandfather, grandfather, tell me the secret of life!"

The old man's mouth wrinkled into a playful smile as he replied, "My child, within every one of us, it's as if there were two wolves fighting. One of the wolves is focused on protecting his territory; he is full of anger, criticism, and resentment. He is fearful and controlling. The other is focused on love, joy, and peace. He is mischievous and full of adventure."

"But grandfather," exclaimed the boy, his eyes wide with curiosity, "which of the wolves is going to win?"

The old man replied, "The one you feed."

Which wolf are you choosing to feed? Every time you think a facet, you are feeding love-consciousness. On many occasions, we choose to criticize, to focus on what is wrong, but every time we think a facet, we are breaking that habit and choosing something totally new.

What we focus on grows. When we start to appreciate instead of criticize, when we begin to perceive the beauty and wonder of the things around us instead of habitually focusing on what is missing, we begin to find love in everything. Then over time, the wolf of fear and criticism inside us ceases to exist and instead merges into oneness with the wolf of love. Over time we come to understand true compassion and merge into oneness with the universe.

True Compassion

Compassion is the highest vibration of love in the human experience. Compassion comes from an open heart, a heart that can see directly through the illusion of separation, a heart that is self-realized.

Are you thinking a facet?

Compassion sees through what is not real, so that all that is left is love. It peels away illusion and self-deception and allows humans to find their own brilliance, their own heart.

Compassion can be soft, and compassion can be fierce. It can move like a whirlwind, destroying everything illusory. We tend to think of love as a sweet, nurturing energy that is blind to all around it. The Biblical story of Jesus driving the merchants from the temple shows that in reality, love can sometimes be fierce. In the story, Jesus arrives at the temple in Jerusalem to find it full of livestock merchants, buyers, and moneychangers. He drives them from the temple, saying, "My father's house is to be a house of prayer. You have made it a place for thieves" (Matthew 21:13). I see this as Jesus exposing everything that isn't based in truth, that isn't based in God, that doesn't vibrate on a high frequency.

This example shows us that love isn't always sweet. Compassion can jolt, and compassion can shock. Compassion can be patient, but it can also be swift and precise like a surgeon's knife cutting away the ignorance that afflicts us.

This is the art of compassion, and there is no love greater than that.

The experience of compassion comes from unity.

Unity

The only way humanity can reach its highest potential—the only way we can experience world peace, unconditional love, and true compassion—is through the experience of unity.

Unity perceives perfection in all of creation, in every aspect of duality. There is no prejudice, there is no doctrine, there are no *isms*—there is just God, experiencing itself in every moment, in the human form.

When God can perceive this, in a human form, she can allow everyone else to realize their own greatness. There is no one to save; there is nothing to protect; there is only to be, to find the perfection of love in all of her creations.

The facets of the Isha System are a natural progression into the experience of love-consciousness. We begin with praise, because praise is a simple choice; it is the choice to appreciate instead of criticize.

Praise love for this moment in its perfection. (Attention: deep in the heart)

It is so easy to appreciate. For example, I have always marveled at my mother. She suffers from many physical disabilities, and her health has been a constant source of discomfort for the majority of her life. But even after sustaining so many losses, so much hardship, she still has the incredible capacity to appreciate all the good that has transpired and to praise everything in her surroundings. She is a beautiful example of the power of praise. When we, like my mother, start to give gratitude for the abundant gifts that are always coming toward us, we find the true beauty of this creation, and everything flourishes and expands, growing beyond our wildest dreams.

In the second facet, we move on to gratitude, gratitude for the love that is everywhere around us:

Thank love for my human experience in its perfection. (Attention: deep in the heart)

When you anchor in the power of love, you realize your own perfection. How could you not be perfect? You are a creation of love. Absolute, unconditional love of self is the most extraordinary experience, and nothing external can take it from you. We celebrate that self-love in the third facet:

Love creates me in my perfection. (Attention: deep in the heart)

Through regular practice of these facets, love-consciousness will become your permanent experience. The more you use them, the more you will find that you are living your days from a place of inner fulfillment and joy. As you come to love yourself, to accept every aspect of yourself, this love will overflow into your surroundings, and you will find that the way you respond to others is also more loving, more supportive.

As we establish ourselves in the experience of love, this feeling intensifies, becoming richer, until it transforms into compassion. With the mastery of compassion, all separation dissolves, and we embrace the experience of unity.

The Fourth Facet

The fourth facet, which completes the three we have already learned, is

Om unity.

What is *om?* The ancient cultures of the world saw that there was an underlying essence that was common in everything, and they found words to describe that essence. In Sanskrit, the mother of all languages, the word is *om.*

Om is the all-pervading vibration of the universe. The sound of om vibrates at the most primordial level with everything that exists.

In the fourth facet, we bring *om* together with *unity.* To vibrate in the depths of om while focusing on the union that exists beyond the apparent separations in the universe brings the brain directly into the quality, feeling, and presence of oneness. The perfect harmony this creates in the mind is then anchored in the heart, resonating at the pinnacle of pure love-consciousness, and radiating that to all of creation.

In this way, the fourth facet complements the other three, grounding the experience we have been developing within the silent depths of union.

Here's how to practice the fourth facet:

1. Sit comfortably and close your eyes, allowing thoughts to flow naturally.

2. Think, *Om unity.* Remember to think it just as you would any other thought, without forcing or straining.

3. As you think the phrase, bring your attention up from the base of your spine to the crown of your head.

4. After thinking the facet, leave a space. After a few moments, repeat the facet and again leave a space.

5. Continue in this way for about twenty minutes. You can glance at your watch or a clock to check the time.

Entering the Silence

Love-consciousness is the most natural thing in the world. When we were children, we experienced it all the time— a peace and joy that accompanied us everywhere. But as adults, we have lost sight of this experience. Our constant yearnings and the underlying dissatisfaction of the intellect are caused by the desire to return to love-consciousness.

The facets focus our attention on love-consciousness every time we think them. By doing this, they bring the silence of our true nature into the forefront of our attention. In the presence of this silence, everything in our life that stems from fear begins to transform, to melt into the peace that is enveloping us.

When we focus on the facets, we follow them into the experience of love-consciousness. We are what we choose. When we choose the fourth facet, our vibration moves toward more unity. As the love grows stronger, the limiting fears that have stained our window begin to fade away. Our perception regains its natural clarity, and we revive the joyful innocence that we had as children. Again, we experience more of our true nature: joy, peace, and silence.

As our experience of love-consciousness expands, we start to perceive the universe in its true magnificence, instead of seeing everything through the concepts, labels, and boxes we have adopted throughout our lives. We begin to relate and respond to our surroundings from the profound silence we are discovering within. This awareness radiates outward, pervading every aspect of our human experience. We see everything more innocently, without comparing it to what has come before. Instead of seeing the name of the thing, we see it as it really is. Instead of seeing what we perceive as "the ocean" we see the heaving, crashing immensity of its presence.

When we first start unifying, we feel this for moments, but then we are pulled out again by our thoughts and emotions or by the changes that are happening in our surroundings. But as we anchor more permanently in the experience of love-consciousness, it becomes increasingly more difficult for the distractions of the intellect to pull us out of this experience of love. Through regular practice, this experience becomes more and more permanent, until there arrives a time when it never leaves.

The Nature of Thought

At first, when you think *om unity,* you may feel peace and silence, or you may not. You may find that your head is suddenly filled with thoughts, maybe even more than usual.

This means that unification is working: it is not something to be avoided. Thoughts come during unification because the elevation of our inner vibration causes everything that does not vibrate on that level to leave. This can include thought patterns, memories, obsessions, and worries.

It is important to remember that unifying is different from meditation. We are not trying to stop thoughts from coming. All kinds of thoughts may come up while you are unifying, and they are all perfect. Never try to avoid your thoughts or judge them as good or bad. The thoughts that arise while you are unifying are part of the process, no matter how entertaining or off-putting they may be.

Don't fight against your thoughts. The intellect is not the enemy. Love your intellect; don't make it wrong. As your consciousness expands, the doubts and tricks of the mind will fall away naturally.

Love-consciousness is much bigger than the intellect—it witnesses the mind and all its machinations. It takes what it needs from the intellect in order to have the human experience, but it has a clear perception of the things that make us suffer. It sees through the thoughts that are based in fear, that make us hold on instead of letting go.

The mind is an endless question mark of permanent doubt. It hazily changes from one opinion to another. It is transient, because it is illusory. The voice of the intellect oscillates from one pole to the other, feeding on confusion and indecision. Complication is its favorite game, as it weaves thought streams into an awkward mess, like a cat with a ball of yarn.

Remember to think the facet: Om unity.

The voice of unity has no doubt. It speaks with absolute clarity, resounding in the silence of your being. When it speaks, there is no question. It is solid and steadfast.

As you unify, the ball of yarn your feline mind has created will unravel in the light of love. While it is unraveling, just let the thoughts flow—they are the bits of shredded yarn that are falling into the dust.

When people begin using the facets, they become aware that the way they have grown up perceiving the world is nothing but a product of childhood conditioning. They recognize for the first time that the world isn't the way they have always seen it—that they in fact *learned* to see it as they do.

This is a stunning realization when it first dawns on you. What once seemed so real now feels like an illusion. As your old way of viewing your life drops away, you begin to free yourself from the tangled web of the intellect. You find yourself effortlessly cutting the branch of your past fears and your doubts about the future.

You begin to fly.

The Freedom of Enlightenment

Once upon a time there was a king. He loved his people and used to disguise himself as a beggar so that he could observe the lives of his subjects without being recognized.

One day, he noticed a young man sitting by the fountain in the park, staring into the distance with a look of serene contemplation. He went up to the boy and asked him what he was doing. Turning his gaze to look at the disguised king, he replied, with eyes so full of love that the king felt overwhelmed, "I am observing my kingdom." Although this response would normally have greatly offended the monarch—after all, it was his kingdom, not the boy's—he was so moved by the deep presence of the young man that he did not know how to respond. He turned and hurried back to his castle in bewilderment.

Over the next few days, the king made sure to always visit the young man during his trips into town. Every time he saw him, he asked him the same question, and every time, he received the same look of deep peace and innocent love, and the same cryptic answer, "I am observing my kingdom."

After much thought on the matter, the king decided that this young man was not an insolent fool but a great sage, and he decided to reveal his true identity to him and ask him to come spend a night in his castle. He wanted to discover the secret of this boy's enlightenment and achieve that same inner experience of freedom for himself.

Upon removing his disguise with a flourish and triumphantly revealing his true identity to the boy, the king was somewhat taken aback by the young man's nonchalant response and seeming disinterest. His incredulity grew when the boy accepted his invitation to spend a night in the castle without the slightest sign of excitement or gratitude.

However, pleased that the boy had accepted, he brought him straight back to the castle in the royal carriage and offered him the most sumptuous suite in the palace. The boy accepted.

The next day, wanting to spend more time near his new-found source of wisdom, the king invited the young man to stay another night. He accepted. Time went by, and the young man continued to indifferently accept the king's generous hospitality. After a few weeks, the king felt obliged to offer him a gift, as was customary in those parts. The boy accepted the fine clothes the king placed before him. And the foreign sweetmeats. And the gold trinkets.

As time passed, the king grew impatient. He had given the very best of everything to the boy, yet the boy had still not revealed his secret to the king! In fact, the boy had hardly even spoken a word to the king during his entire stay. The king began to feel resentful. He started to wonder if the boy really was a sage or if he was just taking advantage of the king's generosity. Out of politeness, the king did not tell the young boy about his doubts, but as the days went by, they grew and grew.

One day, tired of waiting and suspicious of the boy's intentions, the king decided to confront him. He marched up to the boy's bedroom, determined to ask him if he was still observing his kingdom. He was sure that the boy would be doing nothing of the sort—he was probably sound asleep, or lounging around in bed!

Bursting through the door, his chest puffed up with pride, he turned to ask the boy his question. But before he had time to speak, he saw that the young man was staring straight at him with eyes full of serenity. The young man raised his hand and said,

"Wait! I know what you are going to ask me. You have had something to ask me for a long time now, but I am not going to answer. Instead, I want you to go and order your servants to saddle up your two best horses. Today we shall go for a ride."

The king, so unused to receiving orders, and again disconcerted by the young man's piercing gaze, turned and walked out of the room in silent confusion and went to ready the horses.

Down in the stables, the two men saddled up, and the young man set off, galloping so fast that it took the king a few seconds to catch up. At full speed, they raced through the forested valley, reaching the other side faster than the king ever had before. When they arrived at the top of a ridge, the breath-taking view of the enormous kingdom spread out before them, but the young boy showed no sign of slowing. He continued galloping down the other side of the mountain, the king trying hard to match his pace.

They rode for hours, leaving the castle walls far behind. The boy still showed no sign of tiring, and the king, not wanting to appear weak, had to use all his energy to keep up. When they could finally ride no longer, they set up camp by the side of the road, and the next morning, off they went again, the boy racing ever farther from the castle.

For days they rode and rode, through areas of the kingdom the monarch had never even seen before. He silently wondered if they would ever stop riding, but the beauty of the land was captivating, and he began to enjoy the journey.

One day, after many weeks, they came to a fence. The boy went to jump the fence on his able stallion, but before he did, the king cried out, "Wait! I cannot cross that fence." The boy looked around, his eyes shining with joy and inquisitive mirth. "This fence marks the limit of my kingdom," explained the king. "Beyond it, I have nothing. Everything I am is on this side of the fence. I cannot continue."

"That," replied the young man, his eyes burning with the light of life, "is the difference between you and me. Your kingdom is contained within this fence, but mine is in my heart. I take it with me wherever I go." With that, he turned, clearing the fence in one graceful leap, and cantered off, far into the distance.

Part 2

The Diamond Portal

Chapter 5

Opening the Portal

Incorporating the Facets into Your Daily Routine

Now you have learned the four Isha facets:

Praise love for this moment in its perfection.
(Attention: deep in the heart)

Thank love for my human experience in its perfection.
(Attention: deep in the heart)

Love creates me in my perfection.
(Attention: deep in the heart)

Om unity.
(Attention: running up from the base of the spine to the top of the head)

Regular practice of these facets, along with the other aspects of the Isha System, which we will explore in the rest of this book, will bring you to unconditional love of self. They may look simple, but the more you practice them, the more you will appreciate the profound resonance they produce within your being.

These four facets form what I call the Diamond Portal. I call this the Diamond Portal because all humans are like perfect diamonds, and no two diamonds are exactly the same. Our facets are unique, as all diamonds are unique. They have different cuts and different appearances. They are all individual and perfect. They are all translucent and radiate only light.

The center of every diamond is the same. It is pure love, pure consciousness. As light hits the surface and touches the facets, they each display their own unique expression. But the essence, the core is always the same.

Through the brilliance of this Portal, you will discover your own brilliance, but *you* must ignite the fire. You must turn on the light. You must be responsible to yourself, because only you can find the greatness of who you truly are.

The Stabilization of Love-consciousness

One of the wonderful things about these facets is that they can improve your life to the degree that you desire. Many people unify for simple stress relief or to live a more peaceful, enjoyable life. That is fine. For those who seek something more, this system provides an incredibly direct path to the expansion and stabilization of love-consciousness.

What does this mean? Many of you may have experienced moments of absolute fulfillment, in which you felt that nothing was missing from your life. This may have occurred while you were watching children play, during deep meditation, when lost within the eyes of a lover, or just spontaneously, for no apparent reason. Whenever it happens, this experience is usually so fleeting that it is gone in an instant, yet at the same time it is so profound and inspiring that we remember it for the rest of our lives. If you have ever had one of those experiences, you have probably wished you could feel that same feeling of completion all the time.

This is what stabilization of love-consciousness is. It is the permanent experience of inner fulfillment, allowing you to live constantly in a state of plenitude, no matter where you are, whom you are with, or what you are doing. This is true freedom. When your inner state no longer depends on the shifting sands of the world around you, you can live fully, without the need to control or manipulate your surroundings.

Love creates me in my perfection.

> (Attention: deep in the heart)

This is the difference between the Isha System and meditation. Meditation brings you into a state of inner fulfillment, but when you open your eyes, where did that experience go? It's gone. This system, on the other hand, takes you into the experience of love-consciousness and then brings that experience out, into your daily life. You will find that as you continue practicing, the inner peace and joy stays with you for ever-increasing periods of time, permeating every moment of your life until it is always present.

To sit permanently in love-consciousness is to sit in the silence. I call it the "roaring silence" because sometimes it's so silent, it's loud. When you are sitting in love-consciousness, even in the midst of great noise, the silence will be the only thing you can hear.

Love-consciousness overshadows the intellect. It overshadows noise. It overshadows everything. It's within that space that we begin to witness. Within that peace, the frequency of love is found.

There is nothing greater than love-consciousness. It is the only thing that has any true value, because it's the only thing that's real. I can have fame, I can have money, I can be beautiful, but without love-conscious-ness, I will remain an empty vessel; I still won't be complete because my heart will be yearning for something more. Without love of self, attributes like beauty and fame and illusory riches are worthless. *With* the love of self, we can play within the illusion of duality like a child, embracing every aspect.

If our freedom is based in our surroundings, it is tangible but inconstant. It is always changing, and there is always the fear of loss. If our security is in love-consciousness, it is never-changing. It is ever present and infinitely expanding. There can never be loss; there can never be death. There will only be a new stage, with a multitude of different characters playing their parts for our amusement.

There is nothing real but the love. The illusions that we cling to with such ferocity are like clouds that dissolve in the sunshine.

Tips for Correct Practice

We have already established the importance of unifying with the eyes closed for at least an hour a day, but if you want to do it for longer than that, go ahead! Take advantage of your free time to unify—the more you practice, the more you will reap the benefits.

Unifying with eyes closed helps us to connect with the experience of love-consciousness and begin to expand it. Unifying with the eyes open, on the other hand, helps us to embrace the perfection of the present moment.

Every time we unify with the eyes closed, we use all four facets, in order, for approximately equal amounts of time. If we are going to unify for twenty minutes, for example, we will use the first facet for about five minutes, then move on to five minutes of the second, then five minutes of the third, and end with five minutes of the fourth. You can measure the time by glancing at your watch or a clock. Remember, this doesn't have to be exact. This practice never requires any kind of physical or mental effort; nor does it require rigid control.

You may feel more comfortable or more identified with one facet than another. That is normal. However, we always use all the facets when we practice with the eyes closed—the ones we like and the ones we don't like. If there is a facet that doesn't say much to you or maybe makes you feel a little uncomfortable, that means the facet is working; it is hitting against a fear or a resistance from your old belief system. We use the facets to expand our consciousness, not to feel good. Sometimes the practice will feel wonderful; sometimes it won't. That doesn't matter—just keep practicing, and whatever is being removed will leave. When it has left, you will feel much better.

If at any time you feel uncomfortable or find that this process is difficult, just remember: It's within you. It's in you. Wherever you go, there you will be. This process will show you yourself. You may not always like what you see, but you cannot ignore it forever. The quicker you embrace the parts of yourself that you reject, the quicker your discomfort will be replaced with the freedom of unconditional love.

So this is how we are going to practice the facets in our lives: we unify for at least one hour a day with the eyes closed, and whenever we remember, we unify with our eyes open. As you continue to practice, the changes will manifest themselves in every area of your life.

We will now explore some common questions and doubts about how to practice the System correctly. If any of your doubts aren't listed here, see appendix 1 for information on how to receive further support.

FALLING ASLEEP

If you fall asleep while practicing, that is perfect. When we unify, we always create exactly what we need. If your body has accumulated fatigue, you will fall asleep. This is because the body is taking advantage of the deep relaxation produced by unifying to rest and regenerate.

If you are falling asleep a lot and never get to unify, try sitting up instead of lying down. If you still fall asleep, even when you are sitting up, what can I say? You need to sleep!

Sometimes we go through a period when every time we go to unify, we fall asleep. This may last a few days or even a few weeks, but it is a very good thing. When the body has rested enough, you will feel more lively and energetic than ever before. Don't fight against it—just remember you are healing, and it will pass.

POSTURE

When you are unifying, it is important that you be comfortable. That is the only rule with regard to posture. You can sit or lie down, change position, scratch an itch ... as long as you are comfortable.

PRACTICING FOR LESS THAN TWENTY MINUTES

When we unify with the eyes closed, it is ideal to do at least twenty minutes at a time, in order to take full advantage of the deep level of rest that makes unifying so beneficial.

If you are sitting in the doctor's waiting room or in the back of a taxicab, you can still close your eyes and unify for a few minutes, but whenever possible, try to build your hour of daily practice with sessions of at least twenty minutes.

MUSIC

When we are unifying, we are diving deep within our being. Anything that stimulates the senses will only serve as a distraction and should be avoided whenever possible. Don't play music of any kind when you are unifying. However enjoyable it may be, when we are unifying, it keeps our attention focused outward, which is the opposite of what we are trying to achieve.

HEADACHES

If you get a headache during or after unifying, make sure that you are not using any mental effort. Headaches can be caused by trying to forcefully avoid those thoughts that you judge as negative. Remember that this process is not meditation and does not require you to clear your mind of thought or concentrate intensely; nor should you try to control your thoughts. Unifying should feel agreeable and natural to the mind.

Another possible cause of a headache while unifying is dehydration. When you are using the facets, the liquid in your body is being used to release toxins, so it is important to drink a lot of water.

Headaches may also arise as a result of physical stress leaving the body. If this is the case, the pain will pass before long—just continue unifying, drinking water, and getting exercise.

POINTS OF ATTENTION

Sometimes people have difficulty with the different bodily points of attention in the facets. This is usually because they are trying too hard. When we put our awareness deep in the heart, for example, we do not need to visualize a particular color or light. Nor do we have to concentrate in any way. We just bring the attention gently into the heart.

The points of attention open the energy centers in the nervous system, so we can vibrate in ever-higher levels of love-consciousness.

It is very important to commit to doing this practice for a minimum of a month. When we separate ourselves from our surroundings and create the illusion that we don't deserve love, we close off all our energetic centers. These centers are surrounded by stress and toxins. As we start to heal, these stresses and toxins leave, along with the negative belief systems that caused us to protect ourselves from the outside. In order to start energetically feeling the presence of love-consciousness, all this accumulated rubbish has to leave, so we can vibrate on a higher frequency. Some of you will experience the peace and joy immediately, but others will be removing toxins and healing the central nervous system, and this will result in quite the opposite; it will cause incessant chattering of the mind. You might not initially feel the peace and joy. Persistence will allow you to have this experience, and it is well worth the effort. So make this commitment to yourself, and give this system the opportunity you deserve.

Chapter 6

The Seven Components of the Isha System

In its totality, the Isha System provides a comprehensive method for self-healing and the expansion of love-consciousness. Although we have already explored its components within this book, we will now list them clearly, so that you can review them easily whenever you need to.

1. Using the Isha Facets

Praise love for this moment in its perfection.
(Attention: deep in the heart)

Thank love for my human experience in its perfection.
(Attention: deep in the heart)

Love creates me in my perfection.
(Attention: deep in the heart)

Om unity.
(Attention: running up from the base of the spine to the top of the head)

These four facets comprise the Diamond Portal. Advanced Portals are taught on an individual basis, in seminars throughout the world. For more information, see appendix 1.

2. Focusing on Love-consciousness

This step is a natural result of regular unification. As we use the facets and become more and more familiar with the experience of love-consciousness, we find that we can choose that peace, that inner fullness, just as easily as we can choose to think a facet. First we choose to think the facets, and then as the experience expands, we can start choosing to focus on love-consciousness. We continue thinking the facets but start choosing to bring ourselves into the present moment, into the here and now. As we establish our awareness in the experience of love-consciousness, we begin to live life from the depths of our own inner silence.

Using the facets with the eyes open will help you greatly in this step. Every time you think a facet, you are anchored in the here and now. You are choosing to embrace the perfection of the present, instead of choosing to dwell on the habitual thoughts of the past and future.

A practical way to apply this step is by closing your eyes for a few moments in the midst of activity (except driving!) and using the facets to connect with love-consciousness. If you are feeling stressed or lost in the demands of your day, just stop, close your eyes, and go inward. When you feel more anchored within yourself, you can open your eyes again. Continue thinking the facets, and continue choosing that space. This exercise will help you stabilize the experience of love-consciousness more rapidly in your daily life.

3. Feeling Your Emotions

A fundamental aspect of the Isha System is feeling your emotions without judging them. This is quite different from getting caught up in drama or suffering. For example, if we are sad, we allow ourselves to cry. If we are angry, we scream into a pillow, punch a punching bag or mattress, or do physical exercise to move the energy. We do this with innocence, just as a small child would.

A friend of mine was running down the riverbank recently. It's a very serious business, running along the river. Everyone's wearing a heart-rate monitor and constantly checking it. Some people have music plugged into their ears, but the general mood is of focus and seriousness—because exercise is serious, as life is serious, as everything is very serious indeed.

Suddenly a funny little woman came running toward her. Vertically, this woman was tiny, but horizontally, she wasn't tiny at all! Everything that could bounce or move was doing so.

She looked at my friend, and they both began to laugh. The bouncy woman was laughing at herself, and my friend was laughing at her laughing at herself. She was having a great time wobbling up the river-bank and looking comical, and I'm sure she brought a great deal of joy into many people's very serious lives!

A few moments later, a stern-looking cyclist appeared. He looked incredibly focused as he earnestly powered his way up the path. As he was nearing my friend, he suddenly fell off his bike and hit the ground hard. The impact was so shocking it felt like an earth tremor. He'd obviously hurt himself, because his elbows were scraped and his knees were bleeding.

I find it amusing that people's first response when someone falls is often to laugh. I don't know if we laugh because we're embarrassed for them or because we're glad it wasn't us! Then the next response, especially from women, is the motherly look of concern and the frantic question, "Are you all right?" as we try to disguise the fact that we were laughing a moment ago.

124

But my friend didn't have time to respond in either of these ways because the cyclist instantly jumped up from the ground, as if he'd bounced off rubber, and hurriedly checked his precious bike to see if it was all right, which of course it was. He seemed totally oblivious to the fact that his knees and elbows were bleeding. God help us if he'd shown any emotion. Because of course, big boys don't cry.

With her mouth agape, my friend watched him ride off and thought to herself sadly, "He will probably have a heart attack by the time he is fifty." When she told me this story, I wondered how I would have reacted if I had fallen off my bike ten years ago, when I too was a robot. I probably would have had the same response as the cyclist—I would have pretended that in reality nothing had happened, that it was just a scratch and it didn't hurt.

Then I thought about what I'd do now, and I had a very clear vision. I'd be sitting on the ground, crying like a baby, wondering where my assistant was because she'd be able to fix me. Then I'd stand up and kick the damn bike, which was the cause of all my misery. Then I'd probably laugh at myself and ride home.

Remember, when you think a facet, always wait for a moment afterward to let any other thoughts pass. No mental or physical effort is neces-sary—just unify in a gentle, relaxed fashion.

In short, I would have allowed myself to behave like a four-year-old child.

Sometimes when you are unifying, you may feel a deep happiness. Your thoughts will become a distant melody of which you can't quite make out the words, as you are wrapped within the warm blanket of un-conditional love.

At other times, you might start feeling sad or angry, maybe for no apparent reason. This is all part of the process of growth, and it is by no means a reason to stop unifying. As I said before, when we focus on love-consciousness, everything that is not vibrating at a high frequency starts to fall away naturally. This includes all the emotions that we have learned to repress throughout our lives.

How many times have you held back your tears? How many times have you put on a fake smile to hide your anger? In most parts of the world, men are taught not to cry because they have to be strong, and women are not supposed to get an-gry—they have to be gracious and sweet at all times.

We have all learned from a very early age to abandon our feelings, but these suppressed emotions have not disappeared. They lie deep within us, slowly building up until they explode in bursts of rage or drawn-out depressions.

As your experience of love-consciousness expands, your emotions will start to flow more spontaneously. Children are a perfect example of this. They don't hold on to their emotions, so those emotions move very quickly. They are completely present in everything.

When we unify, we are returning to that state of being. We are recuperating that level of consciousness while at the same time living a mature adult life. It's possible. In fact, it's easy. You will see that as your consciousness expands, naturally you will become more innocent, more spontaneous.

Because we have learned to disconnect so drastically from our emotions, when we start to embrace them again it can feel very uncomfortable. It's a new experience for us because we are no longer avoiding our feelings. But it is worth it—finally we will be able to release the accumulated pressure those bottled-up emotions have caused within us.

Sometimes, when we start to release our built-up emotional charge, we think, "Hang on a second. I'm feeling worse than I did before! I wasn't totally fulfilled, but at least I wasn't crying!" If this happens to you, trust that you are not getting worse; it's only that the false mask of your previous so-called happiness is falling away, and you are starting to be real with yourself. This process can be confronting, but the joy that comes on the other side is genuine. It is *true* happiness, and nothing will have the power to take it away from you. You'll begin to wake up happy for no apparent reason, and you will continue to feel naturally happy all day long.

If our contentment can be affected by anything, it is illusory. It is based on our attachments—on other people's approval or on the things around us looking a certain way. When we find true fulfillment within the experience of love-consciousness, there is no fear, because it can never be lost—it is who we are.

Vulnerability is something we tend to avoid at all costs in modern society. We consider it to be a bad word. Yet strength is to be found in vulnerability. Why? Because when we are vulnerable, we are being real. We are being transparent and completely honest. There is great power in vulnerability, the power of truth.

When you allow yourself to be in your perfection, you are giving others the freedom to do the same. You are supporting everyone around you in their own greatness, their own perfection.

All we need to do is be present in the body and one hundred percent vulnerable from a place of innocence. As we let go of the expectations of the intellect and stop judging our human experience, we become divine.

4. Exercising

When we are unifying, it is not only our perception that is changing. The vibratory shift that occurs when we think the facets affects the entire nervous system. The frequency of love-consciousness progressively upgrades the body at the cellular level.

In the presence of a high vibration, any low vibrations naturally become higher. When this happens during unification, everything that vibrates on a low frequency within the body—such as toxins, stress, and physical tension—begins to fall away naturally.

You can help your body remove the stress and toxins that are surfacing by getting some exercise. Any kind of exercise is beneficial—walking, running, dancing, swimming, yoga—any sport or physical activity that you enjoy. Let's try to do a minimum of half an hour per day.

5. Drinking Water

Another way to help the body in its healing process is to drink water. The body uses liquid to flush out the toxins that are being released, and so during unification, it dehydrates more quickly than usual. Because of this, it is important to drink at least eight eight-ounce glasses of water per day. This will help your body eliminate the stress that is leaving. If you are not used to drinking a lot of water, try keeping a bottle on your desk or bedside table and drinking from it every time you remember. In any case, you will find that your body naturally starts asking for water, and you will start to feel thirsty as you become more aware of its needs.

6. Being Real

As the healing process unfolds and the fears of the past dissolve, the masks that previously covered those fears and the behavior patterns we adopted to defend them start to dissolve as well.

We become fully conscious of self, perceiving ourselves and those around us with transparent honesty. Clarity and sincerity grow in our personal relationships—as we open up to ourselves, we embrace the world around us with joyful innocence.

130

The following example will help explain the process of self-acceptance that takes place as we become more authentic:

Imagine that you are an apple with a lovely, shiny skin. Your skin is polished and looks beautiful for the world to see.

That polished skin is like the personalities we present to the world. Our personalities are essentially masks we put on to represent ideals of how we think we should behave and of what we think we should do. These ideals tell us that we should be nice people, that we shouldn't get angry, that we should be successful, that we should be loving parents. They provide us with a billion pretenses about how we should be.

Are you thinking a facet? It's okay to feel emotion.

We walk through our lives pretending to be these ideals. We keep our outer surfaces polished, but the core—the essence of who we are—has a big worm crawling around inside it. This worm has been fed by anger, depression, loss of the spirit, and self-abandonment.

In order for the surface of the apple to be truly brilliant, truly luminous, we have to go in and remove what's not real. That big ugly worm has been swimming around our subconscious, blocking the light of unconditional love that shines from our core.

The facets go in and start to dissolve this worm. They pull it out piece by piece. As the pieces come out, we get to see the lies we've been telling ourselves and the world. We get to see the masks we've been wearing. We get to hear the voices that hold us in limitation. We start to become conscious of self, and at the same time we become conscious of what is not self. The essence or the core of who we are is love-consciousness, which is unlimited, never-changing love. As awareness of our core expands, what we are not also becomes very clear to us; we allow ourselves to see it and to see through it. We allow ourselves to be those pieces of the worm that are trapped within our beautiful core, and then we expel them. We expel each piece that doesn't serve us.

Then the love at our core, which before was over-shadowed by the worm, again begins to shine forth. The flesh of the apple is cleaned, and everything becomes whole and complete. The surface takes on a new luminous brilliance—which is truth, which is natural—because it has embraced every aspect of itself. It has embraced all the parts it didn't want to see.

In order to be divine, we have to be willing to be 100 percent human. We have to be willing to embrace every aspect of ourselves that we judge.

We need to embrace the greed. We need to embrace the fear. We need to embrace the jealousy. We need to embrace the anger. We need to embrace the self-ishness. We need to embrace every part that we've been hiding beneath the falsely polished skin of the apple, so that we can become whole and complete.

A person experiencing love-consciousness isn't a "do-gooder." A conscious person isn't someone who gives relentlessly in order to receive approval. A conscious person isn't someone who abandons her greatness in order to fit in. A conscious person isn't someone who is arrogant, self-possessed, or otherwise masking a multitude of things we perceive to be sins. A conscious person is just an innocent child who lives in each moment 100 percent, giving love to himself and to everyone else, whom he also knows is self. This is the I of union. This is the I of love. This is the I of enlightenment.

The I of the personality, or the ego, is just the fat worm that has been slithering around, munching on the flesh and stopping the light emanating from the core. It's also very important that we love the worm, because he too is love.

7. Speaking Your Truth

In modern society, we have learned to lie all the time. We lie to please others and receive their approval. We lie to defend ourselves, to hide the parts of ourselves we have learned to judge as wrong or inappropriate. We think, "It's just a little lie," but there are hundreds of them! Our greatest fear is to not receive approval. This fear is very strong because we want so badly for people to love us.

When we start the journey back home to ourselves, we start speaking our truth. At first, sometimes you will do it and sometimes not. Often you will be very afraid of doing it, but you need to push yourself more and more to be real, to stand in your own power. To do that, you must anchor yourself in a space of peace and stability—in love-consciousness. Pure love-consciousness is so anchored in unconditional love, so complete within itself, that it doesn't compromise on the outside. It isn't afraid of losing something external, because it knows it's an illusion.

Whenever we lie, we are abandoning ourselves; we are not loving ourselves. Whenever we modify ourselves in order to receive love, we are separated from self. In speaking our truth, on the other hand, we never compromise ourselves in search of approval from the outside.

> *Remember to think a facet. The power is in this moment.*

The truth is like a muscle, the muscle of the heart. The more you flex it by speaking the truth, the stronger your awareness of being truthful will become. Then the truth develops an energy that moves outward, the energy of the heart.

The important thing is to be willing to be human, to be transparent and walk through your fears—for example, the fear of losing other people's approval. Then the muscle of truth begins to develop with great force.

But this is a process. It's not about being rigid. In every moment, push yourself to be more truthful with yourself. It's not easy. In fact, it's very difficult because for all our lives we have done the exact opposite.

I'll give you an example. Once when I was a child, my Auntie Leslie came to visit. She brought her special chicken casserole with her. I don't know what she put in this casserole, but it always tasted rubbery, as if it had gelatin in it, and I found its chewy texture quite horrible. When she was about to leave, my mother said, "Darling, Auntie Leslie is going to visit again soon, and of course she will bring another chicken casserole!" Auntie Leslie was smiling at me, her eyes full of love, as I instantly responded without thinking, "Yuck, I hate that chicken casserole!" My mother glared at me, and I unsuccessfully tried to cover what I had said with a lie. I remember thinking later how much of a contradiction life was. My mother was always telling me that I should never lie, but when I had told the truth, she had looked at me with eyes that could kill. It was apparent in that moment that according to my mother, it was not that we should *never* lie but rather that we should learn when it was appropriate to do so!

As adults, speaking the truth is one of the hardest things for us to do because we think there is something wrong with us—that if we show ourselves exactly as we are, we will be rejected or judged by those around us. So we comply with a general opinion in order to fit in, even if this means abandoning our own truth. As you expand your consciousness, you will see that when you are looking for love on the outside instead of anchoring within, you are separated from yourself. When you speak untruths so that people will accept you, so as not to offend anyone, or to avoid problems, or when you measure your words carefully before speaking, you are separate from yourself.

When I look at the world, I see lots of situations in which people think it's okay to lie because it's been their way of living for so long. As consciousness rises, this will happen less and less because the lies are all based in fear. We feel the need to lie when we are trying to protect something, when we perceive lack, or when we feel the need to defend our images. All these things are illusory, and they are starting to change.

So how do we approach speaking our truth in a manner that is delicate and not as reactionary as my response with Auntie Leslie was? How do we speak our truth when it could hurt someone close to us or threaten our own wellbeing? A colleague recently presented me with some difficult hypothetical scenarios on this subject:

If you were a single mom barely supporting three small children and you disliked your boss and disagreed with his management of the company, would you tell him that, even though you knew you would get fired as a result and have a difficult time finding another job, thereby jeopardizing your children's happiness or even survival?

If your lover had spent ten years writing a novel and he finally let you read it and you thought it was terrible, would you say so?

I perceive these questions to be very valid. As we start to speak our truth and expand love-consciousness, we do not turn into hardened brutes. Quite the opposite, we feel compassion and love for everyone around us. The things that used to annoy us no longer annoy us to such an extent. We tend to speak from our hearts. Lying to people doesn't serve them; it doesn't give them an opportunity to grow. But when we sit with people and speak from our hearts and share how we really feel, initially they might be offended, but usually these truths lead to greater growth, more acceptance, and more opportunities. When people compromise their truth, they create more compromise, resentment, and disillusionment. When people stand in truth, from a place of love, they create more love. When we withhold our truth and instead react, it is usually from a place of scarcity or victimhood, but as we expand our consciousness, we start to create the things in our lives that we need.

So, in the example of the single mother supporting her children, being in this predicament doesn't mean she should let herself be treated as a doormat or think that she can't create something else. Once she started loving herself unconditionally, she would see that she was a powerful creator able to create exactly what she needed. She would realize that the boss might be open to hearing her opinions, and that honesty won't necessarily lead to being fired. In the example of the boyfriend with the bad novel, giving false praise would not give him the opportunity to improve himself and his book and would only strengthen his limitations. Instead, she could compassionately, constructively offer some concrete suggestions for improving the novel. If she spoke from a place of love, her boyfriend would certainly feel it and take her suggestions in stride.

I am very fortunate because I have people around me who are honest. I have occasionally written material that was less than mediocre, but through being open to listen and be supported by others with more experience, I have managed to create something exceptional. Speaking the truth allows people to step into their power. It allows people to go beyond mediocrity, but of course, it starts with you.

Chapter 7

Spreading Your Wings

The Transformational Effects of a Life Lived in Union

As love-consciousness expands, certain traits begin to grow naturally within us. By identifying these traits and following them as guides on the path, we can become more conscious of where we are still choosing fear and where we can move closer to inner freedom.

Enlightened behavior does not follow a rigid moral code or an ethical model, but it naturally chooses those actions that vibrate in love-consciousness, in love. Love-consciousness is love. The only thing it does—the only thing it *can* do—is give love.

The qualities we try to embody in order to become good citizens come naturally with enlightenment. Enlightenment doesn't rob the corner shop. Enlightenment always does unto others as it would have others do unto itself, from a place of unconditional love. Enlightenment doesn't go to war—it could think of nothing more absurd than killing others, thereby killing itself.

Enlightenment never abandons itself by not speaking the truth. It always acts from a place of awareness and integrity.

Humans are seldom in integrity. It takes greatness to stand in integrity within the corruption of modern society. We constantly lie, we wear social masks, we go to war, we steal, we manipulate our loved ones in order to receive what we want, we seduce, we deny our own truth in order to please others, we say "yes" when we feel "no." I'm not saying there is anything inherently wrong with these actions, but we need to discern between what serves us and brings us joy and what doesn't and brings us resentment and suffering. It's that simple.

People often try to ignore the truth within themselves, polishing their apple skin to apparent perfection while the flesh at the core is rotting. Is that integrity? No. That's abandonment of self. That's what causes sickness, depression, low self-esteem, and separation from oneself and from one's surroundings.

> *Think a facet, and see where you are abandoning yourself.*

We all have parts of ourselves that we judge. We've all got secrets, things we think we did wrong, that we reproach ourselves for. It's all rubbish. It's not true. You have never done anything wrong. Never. You are just having an experience, and you can make new choices in every moment. Just say to yourself, "I didn't like that choice. Now I'm going to make a new one."

Finding Love in the Face of Illness

Because of the powerful effect it has on the body, this system has brought some phenomenal results as a cure for illness. I have seen countless cases of immediate and permanent relief from insomnia, migraines, depression, panic attacks, and many other stress-related problems. I have also seen people rid themselves of supposedly incurable diseases.

However, this system should not be used as a replacement for regular medical care. Although the reduction of stress that comes through unifying has been known to bring about great changes on the physical level, the expansion of love-consciousness is not a miracle cure of all diseases. I have also known people who died after learning this system, but they died from a place of greater peace, with much less fear. The Isha System does not necessarily eliminate sickness. It might, or it might not. Some people heal their illnesses; others do not.

Illness is not always a bad thing. It can serve as a wake-up call. Sometimes a close encounter with death can provoke a profound shift in our perception of life. Paulo Coelho's book *Veronika Decides to Die* illustrates this beautifully. It tells the story of a young woman who is told that she is going to die. Through this knowledge, even though it later turns out to not be true, she rediscovers the magic of living.

We will never fully understand why things happen, why people have different experiences, or why people touch each other in different ways, in the hospital or maybe just in line in the supermarket. Things happen for different reasons.

How can we find love in the face of illness? By living perfectly in the moment and by expressing exactly what is going on inside us. By being vulnerable and sensitive, and by not assuming the worst, embracing every second and finding the magic and the love in doing that.

Embrace the love that surrounds you now. If you focus on what you think you're going to lose, you eclipse the light of the present with the shadow of a future moment. Innocence is always the same. If we're innocent, there is never anything wrong in the present moment. We can choose the love or the fear. We can choose to embrace the beauty of what we have, or we can choose to focus on what we are losing.

Here is the story of a woman who practices the Isha System and how it has changed her perception of illness.

I have suffered from rheumatoid arthritis for the past four years. I spent the first two years in bed; the sharp pains that ran through my body were unbearable. I felt alone and depressed, unable to understand why this was happening to me—I was only twenty-five years old, with a baby girl to look after. With the practice of the Isha System, I feel better more often, and when I do, I am able to walk. One day I felt so well that the only thing I wanted to do was to go out and get some fresh air. I found my walking stick and went outside. When I returned, I had walked almost two miles with my walking stick slung over my shoulder.

When the pain comes now, I no longer feel depressed because I know I'm moving forward. Today I continue practicing the Isha System because I am committed to healing myself completely. I have let go of the fear of looking stupid and of expressing my emotions in front of others. I have realized how valuable I am, and how great my being is, to the point that I now give thanks for my illness—it was my arthritis that brought me to find the System, the passport to my own inner wisdom that today is allowing me to choose love instead of fear.

You can find joy in the midst of the most horrific circumstances if you are focused on love. That's where the innocence is. Innocence is a choice that you can make in every moment. It's the choice for love.

Removing Your Masks

In modern society, we have learned to hide ourselves behind social masks of what we consider to be correct behavior. We constantly ignore what we are feeling or thinking in order to receive the approval of those around us.

We pretend all the time in order to be accepted by others, but the irony is that we all do exactly the same thing—everyone else is pretending too. We think we are doing a great job of convincing everyone that "I really like you—you're great" while at the same time we are thinking, "I hate her so much! I never want to see her again!" In reality, we're not fooling anyone—they can all see through our act because they play the same roles themselves!

It takes courage to put down your masks, but surprisingly, when you finally do so, you will receive more approval than ever before, because you will be approving of yourself.

One of the pitfalls on the path of self-realization is the adoption of a "spiritual" mask that replaces the old masks we have learned from society. We get caught up in the intellectual idea of how a spiritual person is meant to look, and we create a *spiritual ego.* Then, because of our outer appearance, our eating habits, our long hours of practice, or our many followers, we consider ourselves to be in a place of enlightenment, when in fact we are not. We create a new box of ideas and rules about how we are supposed to behave, based on the very teachings that were designed to break our boxes!

Absolute completion, or enlightenment, doesn't have a box. It is unlimited totality—it just keeps expanding and expanding, eternally.

This system brings your attention back to your own heart. As you use it, you will realize that it removes everything that is not real. It takes the power away from the root of suffering and replaces it with love-consciousness. Until we've destroyed the root of our suffering, we are just covering it with social masks.

In order to truly behave like Jesus, for example, you have to be Jesus. It is no good just following a set of rules because those rules are not your experience. You're just playing a part, being a character, but that character is not you. To be divine, you have to allow yourself to be absolutely human. To be divine, you have to *become* the Isha facets. To be complete, you have to rise above the matrix of the mind.

Our masks make us feel safe and comfortable, but comfort is one of the greatest causes of our discontent. We think our masks and the comfort they bring make us happy, but in reality they cause us to stop growing as individuals, leaving us stifled and dissatisfied. Our masks make us rigid and static. They suck the spontaneity, flexibility, and growth out of life. The greatest aspect of the human experience is evolution, to become more—more excellence and ultimately more love. Until we cast off our masks, we cannot truly evolve.

Thank love for my human experience in its perfection.

(Attention: deep in the heart)

I love to watch gauchos train their horses. They always push the horses to evolve, to go beyond their limitations. They never allow them to be comfortable within their fears. I remember watching one of them coax a young filly into the ocean. At first she was afraid. She didn't want to go into the water. The ocean is enormous—she had never seen anything like it before, and it was frightening. But the gaucho gently persisted, insisting that she go in. She stuck a hoof in and started to pound the water, trying to understand what it was. Then finally she stepped in with all four hooves. Immediately, the water lost its aura of dread. It became her playground. She splashed and danced, sticking her head in, throwing the water up in the air. It was a delight. This is often the consequence of life. We perceive something new as dangerous, but if we jump into the experience, diving into the depths of the unknown, we find many wonderful new playgrounds.

This is what it means to be unlimited, to be open to receive. As we push all our walls down, opening our minds and allowing our hearts to adventure into the unknown, this creation called life becomes the greatest theme park in existence. It is within the uncertainty of the unknown that we truly start to live. Within our comfort we only become stagnant, fat, and bored. Until we walk through our fears, we will never know what joys await us on the other side.

The following story of a student of the Isha System illustrates perfectly the freedom that comes from removing our masks:

> I started living at the age of forty. Until then, I had been on automatic pilot, completing the functions that had been selected for me by my family, the society I lived in, and the beliefs I

had adopted about what life should be like for a woman of those times.

It was socially understood that in order to be complete, I had to get married, have children, and earn a degree, while at the same time balancing a successful career and social life. It was taken for granted that I would be able to maintain all this in perfect harmony, without complaint.

My desire to conform to these expectations was driven by a profound emotional charge. Since childhood, I had tried desperately to receive the approval of those around me, and in order to get it, I was capable of extreme self-compromise. Time converted these tendencies into subconscious habits. For example, I learned that in order to be loved and accepted, I should never cry or feel jealous. Another habit I adopted was lying compulsively in order to make myself appear more interesting.

Until the age of forty, I lived safely within the illusion that I was successfully completing my responsibilities, inserting myself comfortably into the society that I lived in. I had three children with my husband, and marital life was a peaceful dream without tears or jealousy. On top of my career training mathematics professors at the local university, I led an intense social life, due to my husband's profession in the military. My days were hectic, and it was a constant battle to maintain everything in order. But within all this doing, I had lost all notions of who I was and what I really wanted.

Then everything changed. I received a brutal wake-up call, as if suddenly the light had been switched on and the aspects of my world that had been cloaked in shadows came to the surface. I discovered my husband's infidelity with a very close friend of ours. When he found himself exposed, he countered with surprised innocence, telling me that this kind of thing had been going on during all eighteen years of our marriage, as if it had been a normal part of our lives. He explained to me gently, as one might tell a young child, that these affairs had not affected our peaceful marital life in any way—because fortunately, I was not the jealous type.

I remained in a state of shock for a short time. Then I began to try different therapies in order to come to terms with my new reality. I started to ask myself some questions, very important questions that I had never asked myself before: What do I want for my life? What am I living for? What do I want to achieve in order to feel that life is worth living?

I became aware of the masks I had been wearing for so long. It dawned on me that the man with whom I had spent the past eighteen years was a perfect stranger to me, as were my parents, my brothers, and my children. I was also a perfect stranger to all of them, and worst of all, I was a stranger to myself. I was not the only mask maker. We all were. Our masks were so elaborate that they had even fooled ourselves.

I began to realize that what we saw on the surface of life was not reality, that there must be something essential that united us all, something infinite and marvelous that for some reason we thought should remain hidden and protected. To hide and protect it was why we used the masks. In that moment I knew I had to find out what that something was, and so the search for my essence began.

I started by questioning the different aspects of my life. I realized that I was not fulfilled in my career. I was training people who didn't have the vocation to teach and were only there because it was the only option in higher education available to them. I thought to myself, "These people are the ones who are going to teach math to our youth? Now I see why kids hate math so much!" I left my job.

Then I turned to my body. I realized that my body weight was excessive. On top of that I had calcium deposits in my joints and many aches and pains. I realized that despite extensive conventional treatment, my health had steadily deteriorated. I began to explore alternative medicine and homeopathy, and I became a vegetarian.

These changes in my daily life were driven by my internal search. I walked many spiritual paths, including Christian metaphysics, Silva Method mind control, and the teachings of Marla from Mexico. I also learned to meditate and do yoga, tai chi, and many other practices.

Seven years after discovering my husband's infidelity, I asked myself if I wanted to share my old age with someone who no longer shared any of my interests. By this point, the only things I shared with him were our parental obligations. The new paths that I had begun to explore had brought me to realize that we had little else in common. We didn't even eat the same things! The answer to my question was an emphatic "NO!" and I filed for divorce.

My search continued, but I started to feel the effects of aging. I still had calcium deposits in my joints, and although they hadn't worsened,

152

they greatly limited my mobility. I tried to learn Zen meditation, but it was impossible for me to sit correctly on the meditation stool. Other disciplines had postural requirements that I couldn't complete either. For example, I could not sit in lotus position or keep my back straight for long periods of time.

I learned Reiki, Healing Touch, and other techniques, which I enjoyed immensely as a way to give to others, but I still continued to search for my essence. At age sixty, I had spent twenty years searching, and I still felt a lifetime away from my goal.

I started to lose hope of ever finding what I was looking for. I finally found refuge in *A Course in Miracles.* The only problem was that I didn't understand it! But even though the text was too heavy for me, I practiced the exercises regularly.

I decided that I wasn't going to do any more courses in *A Course in Miracles,* as the book itself said that in order for me to understand it, the only requirement was "good intention, and the Holy Spirit will help you understand." So I refrained from taking any courses in which someone would try to explain to me what the Holy Spirit wanted me to understand. In this way three years went by, and every day I continued deteriorating physically, falling deeper into the trap of my mental inertia.

The Isha System came into my life in an indirect and unexpected fashion. One of my nieces was living with me. She was very depressed, and one of her therapists recommended that she learn the Isha System. The changes in her were dramatic and rapid. The System healed her insomnia and bad moods so quickly that sixteen members of my family, including myself, took part in the next course that was taught in our area.

The first surprise I had in the course was very agreeable: the facets were so easy to practice! They didn't require difficult postures, and the only way to do them wrong was not to do them at all. In that moment I realized that in all the spiritual paths I had walked, I had always had the impression that I was doing it wrong, even aside from the difficult postures. Everything to me had been so complicated, and my fear of making a mistake inhibited my progress. It was wonderfully liberating to find a system so simple but yet so profound in terms of experience. What a relief.

I was sixty-two when I learned the Isha System. If the search for my life's meaning had begun at the age of forty, the encounter with that meaning began at sixty-two.

As I dove deeper into the practice, I began to realize that while walking through the spiritual world, I had only replaced one belief system with another. In addition to repressing feelings of sadness and jealousy, I had added anger to the list of unacceptable emotions, as I had mistakenly understood that a spiritual person does not get angry but instead must forgive everyone without question.

It became obvious to me that my new set of belief systems was even more rigid, even more meticulous, suffocating, and time-consuming than the one I had before. I had left a detention center only to enter a maximum-security prison. This rigidity made me even more judgmental of others, sitting upon my pedestal of self-righteousness. But the Isha System very rapidly released me from my prison, by showing me the door to absolute freedom.

After a few months of intense practice, I found myself able to do yoga exercises that before I was incapable of. My body had become surprisingly more agile and flexible.

I surrendered to practicing the facets in the way that Isha recommended. I let go of the practices that I had previously accepted, including strict dietary routines, the use of aromatherapy and music, and a specific orientation of the head during prayer.

My repressed emotions started to surface. The river of tears that had accumulated over decades began to flow torrentially. Memories surfaced that brought up jealousy, rage, and other feelings I had tried to bury, and I allowed myself to feel them and then move beyond them.

The need for approval was still very strong within me. Even though I had begun to realize that my habit of lying and inventing stories was based in fear, I continued doing so. One of my fabricated stories was of an imaginary romance that I claimed to have had when I was forty-eight, with a twenty-four-year-old. In this story, I had taken a tiny piece of reality and added a huge amount of fantasy. It included romantic episodes that entertained my friends a great deal.

As I continued healing, it became increasingly uncomfortable for me to not speak my truth. When I finally admitted that the affair had never happened, one of my close friends got very upset with me. Yet by confronting her disapproval, I was able to heal my own need for approval. It was worth it.

After a year of practicing the System, I looked back and was astonished to see the changes I had undergone. I didn't understand how something so simple could work so well. I had previously practiced yoga, tai chi, and meditation and had eaten in a much healthier way. I had also followed a strict prescription of quantum medicine. Yet while these previous attempts had only been partially successful, this system was completely healing my life. The calcium deposits in my joints had totally disappeared, and I could now bend and move my hands and feet. I had lost twenty-six pounds, which eight years later, I have still not gained back. I could feel my emotions without judging them, and every day I was more "real." I had taken off many masks and had revealed the lies of my stories. Every mask that fell away and every secret I revealed freed me even more. Now my natural joy had no hidden sadness.

But although these physical and emotional gains on their own would have been sufficient to consider the Isha System worth practicing, my greatest gain has been the immutable peace that stabilized more and more within me. I live every day in the present moment. I'm not attached to anything in the past, and every time I observe something I am attached to, I can quickly release it. I still enjoy living in comfortable surroundings, but my happiness no longer depends on it. I'm also not worried about the future. I now feel like a creator instead of a victim. I know that any situation that comes into my life is a gift for my growth.

On my return to the world I had left behind, the first thing I did was open *A Course in Miracles* to a random page. I started reading, and I was able to understand it. Then I thought, "Maybe that page was particularly easy." So I repeated the process several times. Everything was so clear! I was able to prove what I had heard Isha say, that her system would bring us to understand the experiences that masters such as Jesus speak of.

I was also able to observe the contrast between my lifestyle and those of others in my age group. I noticed that what makes us age is our minds. Most of the people of my age that I came into contact with yearned for the past and the memories of their youth, as if they considered the best part of their lives to be behind them. I can now say with pride that I have accumulated seventy years of youth. Now I live in surrender, embracing life. I accept and enjoy every moment in its perfection. I don't need anything; I am not waiting for anything. In every moment I have everything. This has converted my golden years into the fullest part of my existence. I have destroyed the greatest limitations of aging: fear and resistance to change.

I no longer need to look for love outside myself. Now the unconditional love, the very essence of my search, is here, forever.

Nonattachment

Nonattachment is considered to be the great spiritual ideal for many modern-day seekers, yet more often than not, it is confused with abandonment. In order to achieve enlightenment, people think they need to *abandon,* to *lose,* to *renounce.* For example, they feel they have to give up their material wealth and live in a state of poverty, or maybe leave their families or loved ones to live in a state of chastity, perched on top of a cold mountain, eating nothing but rice. This implies that our modern lives are in some way contrary to the experience of internal love, and because of this, there is a great deal of fear associated with nonattachment.

True nonattachment is about finding fulfillment within ourselves and ceasing to cling to things from a place of fear, suffering, and need. When we achieve this, we finally free ourselves from manipulating, controlling, and other fear-based responses that have nothing to do with love.

You can be a multimillionaire with a wife, a family, and a successful career and still be nonattached—these external circumstances in themselves will not stand between you and inner freedom—but to become enlightened, your highest focus has to be on the union with yourself. You don't have to go and live in a cave in the Himalayas to achieve it—in fact, that won't serve you at all, because as soon as you step back into the world, you will find that your attachments are right where you left them!

Love creates me in my perfection.

(Attention: deep in the heart)

It's not the presence or absence of things in your life that matters—it's whether you're attached to them or not. Let go of all negative belief systems and false ideas, and embody your greatness in every moment. Relinquish control and find fulfillment inside. Always be love-consciousness in action. Anchor deep within, and move through life with awareness.

Nonattachment is something that happens naturally through the expansion of love-consciousness. It is not something we have to strive for. As we begin to find completion within ourselves, our need to hold on to the people or possessions that used to make us feel secure falls away. Only then can we truly enjoy the things we have around us, for we are finally free from the underlying fear of loss. In the following story, one of my students tells of the freedom he has found from his attachment to the search for fame and recognition.

I have been an actor for over thirty-five years. My passion for creating new personalities kept me on the lookout for exciting and challenging projects. When I began appearing on television, my economic situation changed dramatically. I made a lot of money and achieved wide recognition.

Doors opened for me everywhere: there was nothing I could not achieve. But as time went by, I began to identify with the character I had created. In retrospect, I see that I never valued myself, that my apparent security depended completely on my status, on "being someone." Inside, I was scared to death, insecure, and unhappy. Desperate for love and approval, I cowered behind the fragile mask of success and apparent satisfaction. In reality, I was totally disconnected from myself, hypnotized by the false appearance of happiness and success.

Beneath the surface lay my heart, abandoned and forgotten. But soon, it began to call to me. At first it was so soft, I could hardly hear it, but with time, its voice grew louder. This inner voice is what brought me to the Isha System.

Now my life is dedicated to awakening. The path I travel is bringing me closer to this desire.

I now feel such love, a love that stems from the simple joy of being alive, of embracing myself exactly as I am, in my own unique perfection. I have never felt this before. But I have always, always been searching for it.

Letting Go of Addictions

Addictions are a form of attachment. They are an attempt to relieve ourselves momentarily from the inner suffering caused by our need for approval and fear of abandonment.

We can see addictive behavior not only in people but in nature as well—in the mating behavior of stallions, for example. There is nothing more majestic than the magnificent dance of desire that a stallion displays for a mare. He roars and prances, rearing and screaming, arching his neck, throwing his mane. If he were a dragon, smoke would billow from his flared nostrils. Sweat covers his heaving body until he is as dark as a starless sky. His passion is so consuming that he loses sight of all other objectives—he never tires, and he doesn't sleep or eat. He feels no pain—he is obsessed.

How often do we do the same? We abandon ourselves, lost in the self-inflicted torment of desire and addiction. It's all very romantic, but the truth is, the more obsessive we become with something on the outside, the less we can tolerate being with ourselves.

When you see yourself obsessing about something, it's an ideal time to stop and think, "Where am I not loving myself?" Then go inward, find the place of emptiness, and use the facets to fill it with love-consciousness. Have a love affair with yourself.

We all have addictions. There is not a human alive who doesn't have some sort of addiction. It could be to alcohol, to work, to candy, to romance, to sex, to control, or to cigarettes. Addictions are not bad in themselves. You just have to see through them. You just have to ask yourself, "Is this really giving me what I want?"

The point is, are you attached to the experience? Because irrespective of what you are addicted to, the problem is not the behavior itself but your attachment to that behavior.

As we expand our consciousness, the satisfaction we receive from our addictions starts to diminish, and we realize that the things we desire the most are usually the things that bring us the most suffering.

In the following story, a practitioner of the Isha System shares how she managed to heal profound addictions through loving herself.

As a child, I suffered deeply for the injustices I perceived in the world. At age fourteen, I discovered that drinking alcohol helped me feel better. By the time I was sixteen I was taking illegal drugs, and the pain seemed to diminish. But after seventeen years of numbing my heart, I was so desperate that I knew I had to do something different. My drug consumption had escalated out of all control. I only wanted to be alone with my drugs, and nothing—not even my daughter, my partner, or my profession—meant as much to me as my next high.

When I learned the Isha System, I began to experience an authentic happiness and luminosity deep within myself. I had finally found something that I preferred to my old habit of taking drugs! I then decided to go to Narcotics Anonymous to finally put a stop to my drug consumption.

Today I have been clean for over a year—fourteen months and fifteen days, to be precise. Only three percent of the addicts that go to Narcotics Anonymous get through a year without falling back into their addiction, and I am one of them. Why didn't I revert? How did I manage it, when for so many years I couldn't even get through a day without getting high? I was destined to die of an overdose, that's the way I saw it. I was a lost cause. But practicing the Isha System has kept me alive, clean, and happy.

Now I appreciate myself as a mother. My daughter enjoys my company, and I enjoy hers. I feel good about who I am. I am no longer a problem for my family, for society, or for the planet. I am no longer a problem for myself ! I am part of the solution.

Suffering comes from need. We feel that without a particular thing, we are not complete or fulfilled, but as with any false god or drug, what goes up, must come down: when the drugs leave the system, we feel sick. The high is always followed by disillusionment and the need to acquire that feeling again.

Through the practice of the Isha System, love starts to expand, and our addictions begin to fall away naturally. As the nervous system elevates its frequency, the body starts to reject the substances or behaviors we're addicted to because in order to carry the truth—in order to move into love-consciousness—it must heal and upgrade.

As love-consciousness rises, our addictions fall away, and if we try to hold on to them, we finally see that we are only prolonging our suffering. Of course, in the old days, when we used to be robots, we could simply swap one addiction for another, but now that life has begun showing us ourselves, we can no longer ignore the truth. We have to start letting go and finding fulfillment within.

This can be frightening and can make us feel insecure because it's like jumping into an unknown void. Yet once we jump, the rewards are unlimited because that leap of faith is always met with unconditional love. That leap of faith allows the branch that we're clinging to—the branch of fear—to dissolve.

Om unity.

(Attention: running up from the base of the spine to the crown of the head)

For when you jump into that void, you fly.

The Opportunity of a Lifetime

Most of us experience moments of happiness in our lives; many look back on what has gone before and feel great satisfaction. Yet deep within lies the endless yearning to unlock the secret of who we really are, to find true freedom from suffering, addiction, and loss.

Many of us experience loving relationships as well as others that end in drama and discontent. For brief moments we experience what we might call love, but it is often so full of attachment that in reality it has nothing to do with love's true nature. Yet we are not even conscious of this, accustomed as we are to this way of life. We are so used to the choices that make us suffer that we don't even realize we are choosing at all. The intellect is so powerful that it convinces us that we are enjoying life like this.

When the facets start to work, we begin to perceive perfection. We become love instead of being robotic, disconnected, walking half asleep through life.

When I remember how I used to live, it seems as if I were in a fog, trying to understand what it all meant. As I grew older, the fog turned into an alcoholic haze, but I was still the same person, doing the same things, mechanically. It is incredible how powerful the illusion is, the matrix of the intellect—it is so powerful that it manages to suffocate God. We continue to repress ourselves and hold on to our fears, until we reach a point where we can stand it no longer.

Then something happens, always. We get sick or we lose a loved one—something happens so that the pressure can be released, and we stop doing what we did before, and start making new choices.

Once there was a monk who desperately wanted to get enlightened. He went up to his master and said, "Master, what do I have to do in order to get enlightened? I'm willing to do anything!"

The master said, "That's easy! The only thing you have to do is go to the river down in the valley. Along the riverbank, you will see that there are thousands of stones. They are all cold, except one—one of the stones is hot. If you bring me the hot stone, you will become enlightened."

The monk was a very intelligent man, and he decided that in order to not pick up the same stone twice, he would pick up a stone and feel it, and if it was cold, he would throw it into the river. That is what he did. He picked up a stone, felt that it was cold, and threw it into the river. Then he picked up another stone and felt that it was cold, so he threw it in the river. Again, he picked up a stone, felt that it was cold, and threw it in the river.

The monk did this all day every day, for thirty years.

Until one day he picked up a stone...

Felt it.

It was hot!

And out of sheer habit, he threw it in the river.

The system I have shared with you in this book is a very hot stone. Don't discard it out of habit and throw it automatically in the river. This system is experiential, and in order to live its full benefits, you must give it the opportunity to do its work.

What this system promises is the opportunity to experience unconditional love of self. To experience heaven on earth, to be surrendered in every moment and flowing with the changes of the universe. To live in the here and now, embracing the abundance, the beauty, and the magic of life. To perceive the perfection of your creation, and *enjoy its duality*—its inconsistencies, its humanness, every one of its infinite unique facets. As you change your perception, you will find that this human experience can become the most exciting, wonderful, inspiring, enlightening game that has ever existed.

Humanity can be complex, entertaining, beautiful, annoying, unbearable, delightful, fascinating, dull, creative, and artistic. I see it all as a massive potpourri, which I throw up in the air and gobble up like popcorn as it falls to the ground. Life is a game, full of wonderment, and nature is my playground. I revel in the beauty of the planet. I love the magnificence of the Andes, the arid Chilean deserts, the palm-encrusted beaches of Brazil, the lush jungles of

Colombia, and the rolling green hills of Australia. I love the might and perfection of animals—from the comical appearance of the platypus and the wombat to the majesty of a perfectly chiseled thoroughbred horse. I love the scrawny alley cat that looks like a walking infection, and I love the majesty of the black jaguar that slinks through the rainforest. I'm delighted by the contrasts of the city—I love the noise, the disorder, and the beautiful architecture of the main street as well as the shantytowns perched on mountaintops.

There is nowhere in creation where wonder cannot be found.

Inspiration can come from people of all walks of life, from the Indian mystic Osho to Nelson Mandela to the beggar with the toothless smile on the corner of the street. The creativity of humanity presents itself in countless different forms—through the great poets, actresses, philosophers, and gurus as well as the so-called ordinary people we encounter every day.

The world is full of diversity, and there is beauty to be found in all of it. When you experience union, you will see nothing but perfection. You will no longer experience fear, for you will finally know the greatness of who you are.

Imagine looking in the mirror

and the face looking back at you is someone you truly love.

Just imagine...

With love,

Isha

Appendix 1

Getting Support

If you have any questions about your practice of the Isha System or just feel the need to speak with someone who has been through the process of growth you are starting to experience, visit www.isha.com to get free support.

Although the teachings in this book are complete unto themselves, there are many opportunities to share this wonderful experience with others practicing the System, through advanced seminars and conferences. At www.isha.com you will find extensive information about the Isha System, support groups, and events around the world.

We highly recommend participating in an Isha System seminar for added support for your practice. In this seminar, you may also choose to receive advanced Portals, in order to further accelerate your process of growth.

Appendix 2

"La I" Uruguay

Isha has established an international center for the expansion of consciousness, "La I," on the coast of Uruguay in South America.

From the moment you arrive until the time of your departure, "La I" will embrace you, enveloping you in its bright, open spaces and warm interiors, the perfect place to explore your inner self and dive deep into ever-expanding waves of awareness. If needed, qualified teachers will be available to support you in your process twenty-four hours a day.

"La I" Uruguay offers a new concept in vacations. A visit to "La I" is not about escaping from life or "getting away from it all"—it is about returning, to your heart. A vacation at "La I" is a journey back inward. It is the ultimate adventure—into your being, your essence. We invite you to come and explore your inner depths, to have the perfect holiday romance with the best companion you could ever find...

Yourself.

For more information and for reservations, contact us:

In the United States: (646)688-5232
In Uruguay: (+598)37-36994
reservations@isha.com
www.isha.com

174

Acknowledgments

When a star shines intensely, it provokes a spark of light in the heart of humanity. But when a million stars shine, their light is sufficient to brighten the darkness and awaken the whole of creation.

I consider myself very fortunate, as I am surrounded by a myriad of stars that are constantly radiating their brightness. I want to thank them all for collaborating with such love in the creation of this book.

To the people at New World Library, who perceive and support my vision.

To Sankara, who worked tirelessly as we tied the threads of this book together.

To Kali, who, wagging her tail, blessed us with unconditional love.

And, most important, my eternal love and thanks to my extraordinary teachers and to my marvelous students who are taking responsibility for elevating the consciousness of humanity through their own inner healing.

About the Author

Isha is from Australia, but since 2000 she has lived in South America, where she has built a large following as a writer and teacher, and an international organization devoted to promoting her work throughout the world. She is founder of the Isha Foundation Educating for Peace; her programs have been introduced to children, businesspeople, politicians, and others from all over the world. She has special programs for prisoners and those with disabilities, and has received support from the Colombian authorities to teach ex-guerrilla soldiers as part of the process of reintegrating them into society. Her website is www.isha.com. She lives in Uruguay.

NEW WORLD LIBRARY is dedicated to publishing books and other media that inspire and challenge us to improve the quality of our lives and the world.

We are a socially and environmentally aware company, and we strive to embody the ideals presented in our publications. We recognize that we have an ethical responsibility to our customers, our staff members, and our planet.

We serve our customers by creating the finest publications possible on personal growth, creativity, spirituality, wellness, and other areas of emerging importance. We serve New World Library employees with generous benefits, significant profit sharing, and constant encouragement to pursue their most expansive dreams.

As a member of the Green Press Initiative, we print an increasing number of books with soy-based ink on 100 percent postconsumer-waste recycled paper. Also, we power our offices with solar energy and contribute to nonprofit organizations working to make the world a better place for us all.

Our products are available

Our products are available in bookstores everywhere. For our catalog, please contact:

New World Library
14 Pamaron Way
Novato, California 94949

Phone: 415-884-2100 or 800-972-6657
Catalog requests: Ext.50
Orders: Ext.52
Fax: 415-884-2199
Email: escort@newworldlibrary.com

To subscribe to our electronic newsletter,
visit www.newworldlibrary.com

Back Cover Material

Let Yourself Take Flight

Imposing no belief system or dogma, the teachings of the Isha System are practical and easy to incorporate into daily life, yet they produce a profound inner transformation. At the core of the System are four "facets"—simple, powerful statements of profound truths. As you use the facets, an abiding sense of well-being and present-moment awareness will permeate your life. Through parables, moving testimonials, and humor, Isha imparts the essential truths that we have nothing to fear and we are all one. This inviting, accessible book will help you live a life of unconditional love, happiness, fulfillment, and peace.

"Shows us how to make the most important choice in our lives: to experience the love that is present in every moment."
—**MARC I SHIMOFF,** *New York Times* bestselling author of *Happy for No Reason*

"This is an important, even essential book.... Isha gives practical ways to release fear's hold over our lives."
—**JAMES F. TWYMAN,** author of *The Moses Code*

"Isha is making an important contribution through her work, bringing consciousness into many diverse communities."
—**SHAKTI GAWAIN,** author of *Creative Visualization*

"There are rare occasions when someone sings the essence of life itself. Isha does this most beautifully and lyrically."
—**C. NORMAN SHEALY, MD, PhD,** coauthor of *The Creation of Health*

Isha is an internationally acclaimed spiritual teacher and the founder of the Isha Foundation Educating for Peace. She travels throughout the world teaching diverse groups, including prisoners, ex-guerrilla soldiers, and troubled youths. Born in Australia, she now lives in Uruguay.

Books For ALL Kinds of Readers

At ReadHowYouWant we understand that one size does not fit all types of readers. Our innovative, patent pending technology allows us to design new formats to make reading easier and more enjoyable for you. This helps improve your speed of reading and your comprehension. Our EasyRead printed books have been optimized to improve word recognition, ease eye tracking by adjusting word and line spacing as well as minimizing hyphenation. Our EasyRead SuperLarge editions have been developed to make reading easier and more accessible for vision-impaired readers. We offer Braille and DAISY formats of our books and all popular E-Book formats.

We are continually introducing new formats based upon research and reader preferences. Visit our web-site to see all of our formats and learn how you can Personalize our books for yourself or as gifts. Sign up to Become A RHYW Registered Reader.

www.readhowyouwant.com

Made in the USA
Las Vegas, NV
23 October 2021